**TEACHER'S PET PUBLICATIONS**

LITPLAN TEACHER PACK
for
The River
based on the book by
Gary Paulsen

Written by
Barbara M. Linde, MA Ed.

© 1996 Teacher's Pet Publications
All Rights Reserved

This **LitPlan** for *The River*
has been brought to you by Teacher's Pet Publications, Inc.

Copyright Teacher's Pet Publications 1996
11504 Hammock Point
Berlin MD 21811

Only the student materials in this unit plan (such as worksheets,
study questions, and tests) may be reproduced multiple times
for use in the purchaser's classroom.

For any additional copyright questions,
contact Teacher's Pet Publications.

www.tpet.com

TABLE OF CONTENTS - *The River*

Introduction	6
Unit Objectives	8
Unit Outline	9
Reading Assignment Sheet	10
Study Questions	13
Quiz/Study Questions (Multiple Choice)	20
Pre-Reading Vocabulary Worksheets	33
Lesson One (Introductory Lesson)	49
Writing Assignment 1	56
Nonfiction Assignment Sheet	57
Writing Evaluation Form	58
Oral Reading Evaluation Form	60
Writing Assignment 2	62
Extra Writing Assignments/Discussion ?s	68
Writing Assignment 3	76
Group Projects	77
Vocabulary Review Activities	79
Unit Review Activities	80
Unit Tests	87
Vocabulary Resource Materials	121
Unit Resource Materials	137

A FEW NOTES ABOUT THE AUTHOR
GARY PAULSEN

PAULSEN, Gary 1939- Gary Paulsen was born on May 17, 1939, in Minneapolis, Minnesota. He is a second-generation American. His father's family emigrated to the United States from Denmark, and his mother's family came form Norway and Sweden. Paulsen's father was a career Army officer, and the family moved frequently. He had few friends and did not do well in school. Due to family problems, Paulsen spent much of his growing-up years with his aunts and grandmother. During these years, he was introduced to books by a friendly librarian, and began reading voraciously.

Paulsen attended Bemidjii College from 1957-1958. He paid his tuition by working as a trapper for the state of Minnesota. From 1959-1962 he worked with missiles in the United States Army. Upon his release, he took courses and became a field engineer. He worked as an aerospace field engineer from 1962-1966. During this time he read an article about flight testing and thought getting paid to write about things he liked would be a good way to earn a living.

In order to break into the writing field, Paulsen made up a resume. He was hired as an associate editor by a magazine in Hollywood, California. Although his supervisors realized he had falsified the resume, they were willing to teach him about the writing business and he worked there for one year. He also worked as a film extra and a sculptor.

The Special War was Paulsen's first book. It was based on his interviews with servicemen who had served in the Vietnam War. In the next twelve years he published 40 books, 200 magazine articles, short stories, and two plays. His topics included hunting, trapping, farming, and young adult and adult fiction. Many of the adventures in his books come from his own experiences. Paulsen has sailed alone to Hawaii, lived in the northern wilderness alone with only a bow and arrow, and driven a motorcycle cross country.

After he published *Winterkill* in 1977, he was sued for libel. He won the case after a long battle. By this time he was almost bankrupt and had no desire to write, so he returned to trapping predators for the state of Minnesota. During this time a friend gave him a four dog sled team. He took the dogs on a seven day run. At the end of the run he resigned from his job, determined not to kill any more animals. Next, Paulsen entered the Iditarod, the 1200 mile long dogsled race in Alaska. A publisher gave him the money to enter the race and asked to be the first to see whatever writing Paulsen did after the race.

Paulsen published *Dancing Carl* in 1983. This was originally a narrative ballet for two dancers, and a short version was shown on Minnesota Public Television. He published *Tracker*, the story of a young boy who is hunting alone for the first time after his grandfather's death, in 1984. This was followed by *Dogsong* in 1985. Paulsen actually wrote *Dogsong* while training his team for the Iditarod. It is the story of a young Eskimo boy who takes his dog team across Alaska. It was a Newbery Honor Book in 1986. *Hatchet,* the story of a young boy lost in the Canadian wilderness for 54 days with nothing but a hatchet, was named a Newbery Honor book in 1988. Several other books have been chosen as American Library Association Best Books for Young Adults, Notable Children's books, and National Council of Teachers of English Notable Books in the Language Arts.

One of his current works is *Madonna*, a collection of stories about some of the strong women he has known. Other works include *The Foxman* (1977), *The Spitball Gang* (1980), *The Crossing*, (1987), *The River*, (1991), *The Haymeadow*, (1992), and *Nightjohn,* (1993).

Mr. Paulsen continues to write and lives in Leonard, Minnesota. He also gives public reading and performances near his home.

INTRODUCTION

This unit has been designed to develop students' reading, writing, thinking, listening and speaking skills through exercises and activities related to *The River* by Gary Paulsen. It includes nineteen lessons, supported by extra resource materials.

The **introductory lesson** introduces students to one main theme of the novel, using one's inner resources in difficult circumstances, through a bulletin board activity. Following the introductory activity, students are given an explanation of how the activity relates to the book they are about to read.

The **reading assignments** are approximately thirty pages each; some are a little shorter while others are a little longer. Students have approximately 15 minutes of pre-reading work to do prior to each reading assignment. This pre-reading work involves reviewing the study questions for the assignment and doing some vocabulary work for 8 to 10 vocabulary words they will encounter in their reading.

The **study guide questions** are fact-based questions; students can find the answers to these questions right in the text. These questions come in two formats: short answer or multiple choice. The best use of these materials is probably to use the short answer version of the questions as study guides for students (since answers will be more complete), and to use the multiple choice version for occasional quizzes. It might be a good idea to make transparencies of your answer keys for the overhead projector.

The **vocabulary work** is intended to enrich students' vocabularies as well as to aid in the students' understanding of the book. Prior to each reading assignment, students will complete a two-part worksheet for approximately 8 to 10 vocabulary words in the upcoming reading assignment. Part I focuses on students' use of general knowledge and contextual clues by giving the sentence in which the word appears in the text. Students are then to write down what they think the words mean based on the words' usage. Part II gives students dictionary definitions of the words and has them match the words to the correct definitions based on the words' contextual usage. Students should then have an understanding of the words when they meet them in the text.

After each reading assignment, students will go back and formulate answers for the study guide questions. Discussion of these questions serves as a **review** of the most important events and ideas presented in the reading assignments.

After students complete extra discussion questions, there is a **vocabulary review** lesson which pulls together all of the separate vocabulary lists for the reading assignments and gives students a review of all of the words they have studied.

Following the reading of the book, two lessons are devoted to the **extra discussion questions/writing assignments**. These questions focus on interpretation, critical analysis and personal response, employing a variety of thinking skills and adding to the students' understanding of the novel. These questions are done as a **group activity**. Using the information they have acquired so far through individual work and class discussions, students get together to further examine the text and to brainstorm ideas relating to the themes of the novel.

The group activity is followed by a **reports and discussion** session in which the groups share their ideas about the book with the entire class; thus, the entire class gets exposed to many different ideas regarding the themes and events of the book.

There are three **writing assignments** in this unit, each with the purpose of informing, persuading, or having students express personal opinions. The first assignment is to **inform**: students will give information about a nonfiction topic related to the novel. The second assignment is to **persuade**: students will develop a "Brian Robeson" survival product and design a magazine advertisement for it. The third assignment is to express a personal **opinion**: students will discuss an experience that changed them.

The **nonfiction reading assignment** is used as Writing Assignment 1. Students are required to read a piece of nonfiction related in some way to *The River*. After reading their nonfiction pieces, students will fill out a worksheet on which they answer questions regarding facts, interpretation, criticism, and personal opinions. They will also write a short report about the information they researched. During one class period, students make **oral presentations** about the nonfiction pieces they have read. This not only exposes all students to a wealth of information, it also gives students the opportunity to practice **public speaking**.

The **review lesson** pulls together all of the aspects of the unit. The teacher is given four or five choices of activities or games to use which all serve the same basic function of reviewing all of the information presented in the unit.

The **unit test** comes in two formats: all multiple choice-matching-true/false or with a mixture of matching, short answer, and composition. As a convenience, two different tests for each format have been included.

There are additional **support materials** included with this unit. The **unit resource section** includes suggestions for an in-class library, crossword and word search puzzles related to the novel, and extra vocabulary worksheets. There is a list of **bulletin board ideas** which gives the teacher suggestions for bulletin boards to go along with this unit. In addition, there is a list of **extra class activities** the teacher could choose from to enhance the unit or as a substitution for an exercise the teacher might feel is inappropriate for his/her class. **Answer keys** are located directly after the **reproducible student materials** throughout the unit. The student materials may be reproduced for use in the teacher's classroom without infringement of copyrights. No other portion of this unit may be reproduced without the written consent of Teacher's Pet Publications, Inc.

UNIT OBJECTIVES *The River*

1. Through reading *The River* students will analyze characters and their situations to better understand the themes of the novel.

2. Students will demonstrate their understanding of the text on four levels: factual, interpretive, critical, and personal.

3. Students will practice reading aloud and silently to improve their skills in each area.

4. Students will enrich their vocabularies and improve their understanding of the novel through the vocabulary lessons prepared for use in conjunction with it.

5. Students will answer questions to demonstrate their knowledge and understanding of the main events and characters in *The River*.

6. Students will practice writing through a variety of writing assignments.

7. The writing assignments in this are geared to several purposes:
    a. To check the students' reading comprehension
    b. To make students think about the ideas presented by the novel
    c. To make students put those ideas into perspective
    d. To encourage critical and logical thinking
    e. To provide the opportunity to practice good grammar and improve students' use of the English language.

8. Students will read aloud, report, and participate in large and small group discussions to improve their public speaking and personal interaction skills.

UNIT OUTLINE - *The River*

1 — Unit Intro; Distribute Unit Materials; PV 1-4	2 — Minilesson: Plot; Read 1-4; Study ?? 1-4	3 — Study ?? 1-4; PVR 5-7	4 — Study ?? 5-7; Minilesson: Foreshadowing Flashback	5 — Writing Assignment #1; Nonfiction Assignment
6 — PVR 8-11; Oral Reading Evaluation	7 — Study ?? 8-11; PVR 12-15	8 — Quiz 1-11; Writing Assignment #2	9 — Study ?? 12-15; Minilesson: Plot	10 — Writing Conferences
11 — PVR 16-19	12 — Study ?? 16-19; Minilesson: Simile	13 — PVR 20-Measurements; Minilesson: Plot	14 — Extra Discussion Questions	15 — Writing Assignment #3
16 — Group Work	17 — Vocabulary Review	18 — Unit Review	19 — Unit Test	20 — Non-Fiction Assignment

Key: P = Preview Study Questions   V = Vocabulary Work   R = Read

READING ASSIGNMENT SHEET *The River*

Date to be Assigned	Chapters	Completion Date
		(Prior to class on this date)
	Chapters 1-4	
	Chapters 5-7	
	Chapters 8-11	
	Chapters 12-15	
	Chapters 16-19	
	Chapters 20-Measurements	

STUDY QUESTIONS

SHORT ANSWER STUDY QUESTIONS *The River*

Chapters 1-4
1. Who was Derek Holtzer and what did he want?
2. What were some of the changes in Brian since his time in the wilderness?
3. How long after The Time does this story take place?
4. What were some of the things that happened to Brian when he first returned home?
5. What was the situation with his parents?
6. How did Brian's mother react to the request?
7. What did Brian think when he saw all of the gear that Derek had packed in the plane?
8. Brian's mother asked him what his main problem in the wilderness was. What was his answer?

Chapters 5-7
1. What did Brian think about as the pilot was landing the plane?
2. What happened to Brian as he stepped out of the plane onto dry grass?
3. What did Brian tell Derek about the gear? How did they solve the problem? What did Derek say about it later on?
4. How did Brian feel the first night?
5. Describe their first night.
6. What did Derek ask Brian to do about his thoughts, and why?
7. What, according to Brian, was everything?

Chapters 8-11
1. Describe the shelter Derek and Brian found, and how they made it livable.
2. How did Brian feel about Derek as they worked on their shelter?
3. What did Brian think about their trip after they had been there three days?
4. What did Derek say was lacking?
5. What did Brian tell Derek about teaching people to survive in the wilderness?
6. Describe the thunder and the events that happened during the storm.
7. What was Brian's plan?

Chapters 12-15
1. What did Brian realize about Derek? How did it affect him?
2. What did Brian think Derek needed, and what happened when Brian tried to give it to him?
3. What did Brian find in the briefcase? What did he decide to do?
4. What was the distance from the lake to the trading post? How long did Brian think it would take to get there?
5. What was Brian's main problem?
6. How did Brian make the raft?

Short Answer Study Questions *The River*

Chapters 16-19
1. How did Brian keep Derek on the raft?
2. What did Brian do just before he started down the river?
3. What did Brian realize about his time estimate?
4. Describe the beginning of the trip down the river, from the time Brian left until the first night.
5. What was Brian's physical condition during the first night? What happened because of it?
6. What was the "bad thinking?" What did Brian do about it?
7. What did Brian find out the next morning when he looked at the map? How did he feel about his discovery?

Chapters 20-Measurements
1. What happened next to the raft and to Brian?
2. How did Brian recover the raft? What was its condition and Derek's?
3. What did Brian do when he found the raft?
4. How were they rescued? What was Brian's reaction to the rescue?
5. What did Brian receiver about 7 months later?
6. What effects did Brian have from the trip?
7. What happened to Derek?

ANSWER KEY: SHORT ANSWER STUDY QUESTIONS *The River*

Chapters 1-4

1. Who was Derek Holtzer and what did he want?
    Derek was a psychologist from a government survival school. He and the two men who came with him wanted Brian to go into the wilderness again, so they could learn from him and teach the students in the survival school.

2. What were some of the changes in Brian since his first time in the wilderness?
    He liked to cook. He became closer to his mother, and admired her. He learned to accept things. He became evasive when talking about his time in the wilderness.

3. How long after The Time does this story take place?
    It takes place one year after he was rescued.

4. What were some of the things that happened to Brian when he first returned home?
    There was a TV special about him. A company put his face on a T shirt. Another company wanted to develop a line of Brian Robeson survival jeans. Someone wanted to write a book about him. He lost his privacy, because the press was following him everywhere.

5. What was the situation with his parents?
    His mother was still seeing the other man, although not as much. His father was planning to marry another woman.

6. How did Brian's mother react to the request?
    At first she said it was insane. She agreed after she realized Brian really wanted to do it, and Derek assured her it would be safe.

7. What did Brian think when he saw all of the gear that Derek had packed in the plane?
    He thought it was too much. It was all wrong to take that much gear.

8. Brian's mother asked him what his main problem in the wilderness was. What was his answer?
    He said hunger was his main problem.

Chapters 5-7

1. What did Brian think about as the pilot was landing the plane?
    He was comparing the landing to his own, realizing how lucky he had been.

2. What happened to Brian as he stepped out of the plane onto dry grass?
    He changed completely. He became what he had been before at the lake.

3. What did Brian tell Derek about the gear? How did they solve the problem? What did Derek say about it later on?
    Brian said if they unloaded the gear, he would go home. They compromised and took their belt knives, a radio, and Derek's briefcase and notebooks. Later on, Derek admitted that Brian was right.

4. How did Brian feel the first night?
    He thought he was insane for being there.

5. Describe their first night.
    They didn't have a fire because they could not find a fire stone. They made a lean-to, but it did not have the protection of an overhanging rock ledge like Brian's previous one. The mosquitoes came and bothered them all night.

6. What did Derek ask Brian to do about his thoughts, and why?
    Derek asked Brian to think out loud so he could record the thoughts in his notebook.

7. What, according to Brian, was everything?
    Food was everything.

Chapters 8-11

1. Describe the shelter Derek and Brian found, and how they made it livable.
    They found a large depression left when a tree fell. It was in a hillside with an overhanging rock shelf. There were large trees on their side. They made beds from pine boughs. Brian found a piece of flint and made a fire.

2. How did Brian feel about Derek as they worked on their shelter?
    He liked Derek more and more.

3. What did Brian think about their trip after they had been there three days?
    He thought it was like a "big happy camping trip." There was nothing to make it rough. They had a fire, food, and shelter. Nothing was wrong.

4. What did Derek say was lacking?
    He said the trip lacked tension.

5. What did Brian tell Derek about teaching people to survive in the wilderness?
   He said it wouldn't work unless each person actually had to try and survive. Just telling them wouldn't work.

6. Describe the thunder and the events that happened during the storm.
   The thunder seemed like it came from inside Brian. It was explosive, and was the loudest noise he had ever heard. When the lightning came, Derek reached for his briefcase and the radio. The lightning hit the radio, entered Derek's hand, and went all through him. It knocked him unconscious. Then the lightning hit Brian, and he blacked out.

7. What was Brian's plan?
   He was going to make Derek comfortable and wait for help to come. He knew someone would try to contact them on the radio in about a week, and he thought he could wait that long.

Chapters 12-15
1. What did Brian realize about Derek? How did it affect him?
   He realized Derek was in a coma. That night he tried to will Derek awake, but it didn't work. Then he felt some anger and resentment. Finally he started to think about what he could do.

2. What did Brian think Derek needed, and what happened when Brian tried to give it to him?
   Brian thought Derek needed water. Derek started choking when Brian tried to give him some.

3. What did Brian find in the briefcase? What did he decide to do?
   He found a map that showed the lake, the river that flowed out of it, and a trading post. He decided to make a raft and take Derek to the trading post.

4. What was the distance from the lake to the trading post? How long did Brian think it would take to get there?
   The trading post was about 100 miles or 150 kilometers from the lake. Brian estimated it would take 35 to 40 hours to make the trip.

5. What was Brian's main problem?
   He didn't have a tool to use to make the raft. All he had were the two knives, and he couldn't use them to cut through the logs.

6. How did Brian make the raft?
   He found a grove of trees that had been chewed down by beavers. He used 8 logs that were 8 feet long. He dragged them down to the lake. Then he used smaller sticks to make cross pieces and put the logs between them. He cut his jacket into strips and tied the cross pieces together.

Chapters 16-19
1. How did Brian keep Derek on the raft?
    He used more strips from his jacket and tied him on.

2. What did Brian do just before he started down the river?
    He left a note in the plastic case with the radio. He tied the radio under the overhang so it would be visible.

3. What did Brian realize about his time estimate?
    It was taking longer than he had originally thought. His new estimate was 50 hours.

4. Describe the beginning of the trip down the river, from the time Brian left until the first night.
    It was difficult. The raft was hard to turn, and Brian often ran into the bank. He learned to paddle through the curves and kept the raft mostly on course. He found that his time estimate was short, and re-estimated that the trip would take 50 hours.

5. What was Brian's physical condition during the first night? What happened because of it?
    He was tired and he would fall asleep between paddle strokes. At one point he fell asleep and woke up to find the raft in a lake. He began paddling out of the lake. He stayed awake, but began to hallucinate.

6. What was the "bad thinking?" What did Brian do about it?
    After two nights without sleep, Brian began thinking that it would be better if Derek were gone. He screamed "No", touched Derek's leg and mumbled that they would go all of the way together.

7. What did Brian find out the next morning when he looked at the map? How did he feel about his discovery?
    He discovered that the lake he had been in was not on the map. He became concerned that if the map were inaccurate the trading post might not be there. Brian realized that his decision to find the trading post might have been foolish.

Chapters 20-Measurements
1. What happened next to the raft and to Brian?
    The raft went through a chute that was like a waterfall. It struck a submerged boulder and Brian flew off. The raft, with Derek on it, floated away. Brian was caught in the pressure wave from the chute.

2. How did Brian recover the raft? What was its condition and Derek's?
    He swam until he found it. beneath some overhanging trees. Derek and the raft were fine.

3. What did Brian do, in order, when he found the raft?
   He made sure Derek was breathing. Then he either fell asleep or was unconscious across Derek. When he woke up he made a new paddle. He paddled all day and all night.

4. How were they rescued? What was Brian's reaction to the rescue?
   Brian paddled until he reached the trading post. A dog there alerted a young boy who ran to the trading post for help. A man and woman pulled him out of the water. He was crying as they helped him. The man jumped in and took care of Derek.

5. What did Brian receive about 7 months later?
   It was a 16 foot Kevlar canoe with paddles. The words "The Raft" were painted on both sides. Attached was a thank you note from Derek

6. What effects did Brian have from the trip?
   He had no long range difficulties. He lost 12 pounds. His hands were infected from bacteria in the lake but they toughened up.

7. What happened to Derek?
   He began to come out of the coma in another week. In 6 months he was fine.

MULTIPLE CHOICE STUDY/QUIZ QUESTIONS *The River*

<u>Chapters 1-4</u>

1. Who was Derek Holtzer and what did he want?
    A. He was a tour promoter from a resort club. He wanted to develop some wilderness tours, and asked Brian to serve as the consultant and spokesperson for the group.
    B. He was an author who wanted to write a book about Brian's adventures in the wilderness.
    C. He was a psychologist from a government survival school. He wanted Brian to go into the wilderness again, so they could learn from him and teach their students.
    D. He was a clothing manufacturer who wanted to make clothes with Brian's name on them.

2. Which was **not** one of the changes in Brian since his time in the wilderness?
    A. He became closer to his mother, and admired her.
    B. He liked to cook.
    C. He became evasive when talking about his time in the wilderness.
    D. He became nervous and jittery in small, closed-in places.

3. How long after The Time does this story take place?
    A. It takes place one year after he was rescued.
    B. It takes place two years after he was rescued.
    C. It takes place six months after he was rescued.
    D. It takes place a year and a half after he was rescued.

4. Which of the following happened to Brian when he first returned home?
    A. He found out his old girlfriend was going steady with someone else, because she thought he was dead.
    B. He had nightmares every night, and woke up screaming.
    C. He lost his privacy, because the press was following him everywhere.
    D. He was afraid to go anywhere without his hatchet on his belt.

5. True or False: Brian's mother planning to marry the other man.
    A. True
    B. False

6. How did Brian's mother react to Derek's request?
    A. She said absolutely no, and told Derek to leave her home.
    B. At first she said it was insane. She agreed when Brian said he really wanted to do it.
    C. She thought it was a good idea, and helped them talk his father into agreeing.
    D. She left it completely up to Brian.

Multiple Choice Questions *The River*

7. True or False: Brian thought it was all wrong to take the gear Derek had packed.
    A. True
    B. False

8. Brian's mother asked him what his main problem in the wilderness was. What was his answer?
    A. He said fear was his main problem.
    B. He said mosquito bites was his main problem.
    C. He said loneliness was his main problem.
    D. He said hunger was his main problem.

Multiple Choice Questions *The River*

Chapters 5-7

1. What did Brian think about as the pilot was landing the plane?
   A. He was comparing the landing to his own, realizing how lucky he had been.
   B. He was thinking about his girlfriend, and missing her.
   C. He was planning what to do when they landed.
   D. He was thinking about taking flying lessons when he got back.

2. What happened to Brian as he stepped out of the plane onto dry grass?
   A. He had a panic attack and ran back into the plane.
   B. He took a deep breath and told Derek he had missed the wilderness.
   C. He changed completely. He became what he had been before at the lake.
   D. He started crying and said he didn't know if he could go through with it.

3. What was the compromise about the gear?
   A. They took all of the gear but Brian hid it where only he could find it.
   B. They took food and a tent, but nothing else.
   C. They took a gun, some flares, and Brian's old hatchet.
   D. They took their belt knives, a radio, and Derek's briefcase and notebooks.

4. How did Brian feel the first night?
   A. He thought he was insane for being there.
   B. He felt right at home.
   C. He was worried that Derek would not be able to make it.
   D. He felt excited and ready to face new challenges.

5. Which of the following did **not** happen on their first night?
   A. They were cold and homesick.
   B. They had a large fire.
   C. They made a lean-to, but it did not give much protection.
   D. The mosquitoes came and bothered them all night.

6. True or False: Derek asked Brian to think out loud so he could record the thoughts in his notebook.
   A. True
   B. False

7. What, according to Brian, was everything?
   A. Bravery was everything.
   B. Sleep was everything.
   C. Food was everything.
   D. Shelter was everything.

Multiple Choice Questions *The River*

Chapters 8-11

1. Describe Derek and Brian's shelter.
   A. They found a log cabin that fur trappers had built. It was in perfect condition.
   B. They found an abandoned bear's den in a large rock.
   C. They found a large depression on a hillside. It was left when a tree fell.
   D. They dug a pit deep in the ground and covered it with pine boughs.

2. How did Brian feel about Derek as they worked on their shelter?
   A. He liked Derek more and more.
   B. He didn't like Derek at all.
   C. He didn't care one way or the other.
   D. He thought Derek reminded him of his father.

3. True or False: Brian thought the trip was going very well after the first three days.
   A. True
   B. False

4. What did Derek say about the trip?
   A. He said it was not as hard as he thought it would be.
   B. He said it was boring.
   C. He said it was going just as he expected, and he was very pleased.
   D. He said the trip lacked tension.

5. True or False: Brian said each person actually had to try and survive to learn how to do it.
   A. True
   B. False

6. Which of the following happened during the storm?
   A. The thunder made them both deaf. They remained that way for several hours.
   B. The wind ripped their shelter apart, picked up Derek's notebooks and threw them into the lake.
   C. Lightning hit the radio, went all through Derek, and knocked him unconscious.
   D. The lake overflowed and drove them out of their camp.

7. What was Brian's plan?
   A. He was going to build a signal fire.
   B. He was going to try and repair the damaged gear.
   C. He was going to continue on with the experiment has they had planned.
   D. He was going to wait for help to come. .

Multiple Choice Questions *The River*

Chapters 12-15

1. What did Brian realize about Derek?
   A. He realized Derek was paralyzed.
   B. He realized Derek was dying from malnutrition.
   C. He realized Derek was in a coma.
   D. He realized Derek had suffered brain damage and would probably not recover.

2. True or False: Derek started choking when Brian tried to give him some water.
   A. True
   B. False

3. What did Brian find in the briefcase? What did he decide to do?
   A. He found a notebook and decided to continue Derek's research for him by writing down everything that had happened since the storm.
   B. He found a second radio that Derek had hidden. He decided to call for help.
   C. He found a map that showed the lake, the river that flowed out of it, and a trading post. He decided to make a raft and take Derek to the trading post.
   D. He found a schedule that showed someone would be calling them in three more days. He decided to continue waiting for help.

4. What was the distance from the lake to the trading post? How long did Brian think it would take to get there?
   A. The trading post was about 100 miles or 150 kilometers from the lake. Brian estimated it would take 35 to 40 hours to make the trip.
   B. The trading post was about 200 miles or 32 kilometers from the lake. Brian estimated it would take 50 to 60 hours to make the trip.
   C. The trading post was about 50 miles or 81 kilometers from the lake. Brian estimated it would take 20 to 25 hours to make the trip.
   D. The trading post was about 150 miles or 243 kilometers from the lake. Brian estimated it would take 45 to 50 hours to make the trip.

5. What was Brian's main problem?
   A. He thought Derek needed constant watching. He couldn't figure out how to watch Derek and build the raft at the same time.
   B. He had never built a raft, and didn't know how to do it.
   C. The logs he found were too heavy for him to lift by himself. He needed help, and he didn't have it.
   D. He didn't have a tool to use to make the raft. All he had were the two knives, and he couldn't use them to cut through the logs.

6. True or False: Brian found an old rowboat in the shallow water near their shelter. He was able to use the wood to build a raft.
   A. True
   B. False

Multiple Choice Questions *The River*

Chapters 16-19

1. How did Brian keep Derek on the raft?
   A. He used more strips from his jacket and tied him on.
   B. He weighted Derek's pockets down with stones to keep him from rolling around.
   C. He tied him on with vines.
   D. He made a glue from pine tar and stuck Derek to the raft with it.

2. What did Brian do just before he started down the river?
   A. He started a slow burning signal fire near their campsite.
   B. He gathered enough food for a week and put it on the raft.
   C. He made a signal marker out of stones and branches to show which way they had gone.
   D. He left a note in the plastic case with the radio and tied it under the overhang.

3. What did Brian realize about his time estimate? How did it change?
   A. It was taking less time than he thought. His new estimate was 25 hours.
   B. It was taking longer than he had originally thought. His new estimate was 50 hours.
   C. It was taking less time than he thought. His new estimate was 46 hours.
   D. It was taking longer than he thought. His new estimate was 72 hours.

4. True or False: The first part of the trip was easy. The raft stayed on course and was easy to steer.
   A. True
   B. False

5. What happened because of Brian's physical condition during the first night?
   A. He fell asleep and fell off the raft.
   B. He was in good shape and paddled almost fifteen miles.
   C. He tried to stay awake and began to hallucinate.
   D. His arms got so sore he could not paddle. He had to let the raft drift.

6. What was the "bad thinking?" that Brian experienced two nights without sleep? What did Brian do about it?
   A. Brian thought it would be better to leave Derek in a sheltered spot near the river bank. He made a small lean-to, and left Derek there while he went for help.
   B. Brian thought he had made a big mistake and they would never find the trading post. He thought about taking his own life and Derek's. Then he realized he could make it, and he kept going.
   C. Brian began thinking that it would be better if Derek were gone. He screamed "No," touched Derek's leg and mumbled that they would go all of the way together.
   D. Brian was too tired to go on. He thought about resting where he was for a day or two. Then he realized he had to get to the trading post..

Multiple Choice Questions *The River*
Chapters 16-19 Continued

7. What did Brian find out the next morning when he looked at the map?
   A. The trading post was closer than he thought.
   B. The map was really for another section of the wilderness, not where he was.
   C. The part of the map with the trading post on it had fallen into the water and was lost.
   D. He discovered that the lake he had been in was not on the map.

Multiple Choice Questions *The River*

Chapters 20-Measurements

1. Which of the following did **not** happen?
   A. The raft went through a chute that was like a waterfall.
   B. The jacket strips that tied Derek came loose and he fell off.
   C. The raft struck a submerged boulder.
   D. Brian was caught in the pressure wave from the chute.

2. True or False: Brian swam until he found the raft beneath some overhanging trees. Derek and the raft were fine.
   A. True
   B. False

3. What did Brian do **first** when he found the raft?
   A. He either fell asleep or fell unconscious across Derek.
   B. He fixed the raft.
   C. He began paddling immediately.
   D. He made sure Derek was breathing.

4. True or False: A man in a motorboat saw Brian and helped push the raft to the trading post.
   A. True
   B. False

5. What did Brian receive about 7 months later?
   A. He received an autographed copy of Derek's new Wilderness Survival Manual.
   B. He received a large check from the government for his work.
   C. He received a canoe and paddles from Derek.
   D. He received an offer to teach at the government survival school.

6. Which of the following is true?
   A. Brian did not have any long range difficulties from the trip.
   B. Brian lost 25 pounds on the trip.
   C. Brian's feet were infected from bacteria in the lake but they toughened up.
   D. Brian's mother sued the government for not protecting her son from danger.

7. What happened to Derek?
   A. He was permanently paralyzed on his right side.
   B. He needed hospital care for another year. he was never able to return to work.
   C. He was fine two days after they returned.
   D. He began to come out of the coma in another week. In 6 months he was fine.

STUDENT ANSWER SHEET MULTIPLE CHOICE/QUIZ QUESTIONS
Scorpions

Chapters 1-4	Chapters 5-7	Chapters 8-11
1.	1.	1.
2.	2.	2.
3.	3.	3.
4.	4.	4.
5.	5.	5.
6.	6.	6.
7.	7.	7.
8.		

Chapters 12-15	Chapters 16-19	Chapters 20-Measurements
1.	1.	1.
2.	2.	2.
3.	3.	3.
4.	4.	4.
5.	5.	5.
6.	6.	6.
7.	7.	7.
8.		

ANSWER KEY-MULTIPLE CHOICE/QUIZ QUESTIONS

Chapters 1-4	Chapters 5-7	Chapters 8-11
1. C	1. A	1. C
2. D	2. C	2. A
3. A	3. D	3. B False
4. C	4. A	4. D
5. B False	5. B	5. A True
6. B	6. A True	6. C
7. A True	7. C	7. D
8. D		

Chapters 12-15	Chapters 16-19	Chapters 20-Measurements
1. C	1. A	1. B
2. A True	2. D	2. A True
3. C	3. B	3. D
4. A	4. B False	4. B False
5. D	5. C	5. C
6. B False	6. C	6. A
7.	7. D	7. D

PREREADING VOCABULARY WORKSHEETS

The River Vocabulary

Chapters 1-4
Part I: Using Prior Knowledge and Context Clues
Below are the sentences in which the vocabulary words appear in the text. Read the sentence. Use any clues you can find in the sentence combined with your prior knowledge, and write what you think the underlined words mean on the lines provided.

1. Brian had a mental picture of the porcupine coming into his shelter in the dark, throwing the hatchet and hitting the rock *embedded* in the wall and getting sparks.

   _____

2. In all his dealings with the new world around him since he was reborn in the woods -- as he thought of it -- he had to be *evasive*, hold back.

   _____

3. As if on *cue* the doorbell rang and she went to the door with Brian following.

   _____

4. "We would control the operation closely," he said, "and take every *precaution* possible."

   _____

5. In all the time since his return, he had had dozens of kids and not a few adults say how much they would have liked to do it -- be *marooned* in the woods with nothing but a hatchet.

   _____

6. But now he *clambered* in and took the seat in back with a relaxed attitude -- it all felt the same and yet different somehow.

   _____

7. Derek had decided he should be the one to go -- even though he had little or no survival knowledge -- because he was a psychologist and that was the *aspect* they wished to learn about.

   _____

8. Brian's mother thought of using the same lake, but Derek *vetoed* it because they wanted it all to be new to Brian.

_____

9. He had to *revert*, to become part of the woods, an animal.

_____

10. But when he came back, and had been back a time, he started to "*rectify*," as he thought of it.

_____

Part II: Determining the Meaning   Match the vocabulary words to their dictionary definitions.

_____ 1. embedded   A. abandoned with little hope of rescue
_____ 2. evasive   B. misleading
_____ 3. cue   C. to return to a former condition
_____ 4. precaution   D. a way of looking at something
_____ 5. marooned   E. firmly enclosed
_____ 6. clambered   F. to set right; to correct
_____ 7. aspect   G. rejected; refused
_____ 8. vetoed   H. a signal or prompt
_____ 9. revert   I. climbed with difficulty
_____ 10. rectify   J. a safeguard

The River Vocabulary

<u>Chapters 5-7</u>
Part I: Using Prior Knowledge and Context Clues
Below are the sentences in which the vocabulary words appear in the text. Read the sentence. Use any clues you can find in the sentence combined with your prior knowledge, and write what you think the underlined words mean on the lines provided.

1. "How about a *compromise*?" "What do you mean?" "We keep the radio in case there's trouble -- serious trouble."

   _____

2. Things began to *disintegrate* fast after that.

   _____

3. "You have to tell me everything, *externalize* it for me, so I can write it."

   _____

4. It was not a thick stand -- it would maybe have been enough for one person, but with two it was *skimpy* --still, there were some and they worked through the brush in their underwear, eating every berry they could find."

   _____

Part II: Determining the Meaning   Match the vocabulary words to their dictionary definitions.

____ 1. compromise   A. to fall apart
____ 2. disintegrate   B. not enough; inadequate
____ 3. externalize   C. an agreement
____ 4. skimpy   D. to show outwardly

The River Vocabulary

Chapters 8-11
Part I: Using Prior Knowledge and Context Clues
Below are the sentences in which the vocabulary words appear in the text. Read the sentence. Use any clues you can find in the sentence combined with your prior knowledge, and write what you think the underlined words mean on the lines provided.

1. He dropped like an *anvil*, his finger still pointing at the fish.

   _____

2. It was then approaching evening, and Brian knew they would need a shelter of some kind and a fire, before dark and the evening *horde* of insects found them.

   _____

3. To this, he added some *pulverized*, dried grass, worked almost into flour, and when it was all together, he gently used his finger to make a hole in the middle.

   _____

4. Then they had *enhanced* the beds and made them deep and soft with more boughs, there was enough firewood for a month, and they had made birch-bark containers to hold extra hazelnuts and berries.

   _____

5. On this side of the lake the forest was more open and the plums and nuts and berries seemed to *thrive* in the light and heat.

   _____

6. Nothing. He turned the *squelch* control down and listened for the hiss of static, but there was nothing. Not even noise.

   _____

The River Vocabulary

Part II: Determining the Meaning   Match the vocabulary words to their dictionary definitions.

_____ 1. anvil   A. to silence
_____ 2. horde   B. ground to a powder or dust
_____ 3. pulverized   C. iron or steel block for shaping metal
_____ 4. enhanced   D. to succeed
_____ 5. thrive   E. a large group; a swarm
_____ 6. squelch   F. improved

The River Vocabulary

Chapters 12-15

Part I: Using Prior Knowledge and Context Clues

Below are the sentences in which the vocabulary words appear in the text. Read the sentence. Use any clues you can find in the sentence combined with your prior knowledge, and write what you think the underlined words mean on the lines provided.

1. Derek was down, unconscious. In a *coma*.

   _____

2. He threw down the stick in *exasperation*.

   _____

3. He felt like he was *prying* and decided not to read any more of the notebooks.

   _____

4. Brian remembered his mother sitting there, his mother smiling. All her questions answered, all her *doubts* gone.

   _____

5. But in the largeness of the country shown on the map, the *massive* forest the map showed, the river was a small thing, and he had negated it.

   _____

6. But in the largeness of the country shown on the map, the massive forest the map showed, the river was a small thing, and he had *negated* it.

   _____

7. He had gone back twice to check on Derek while working and now that it was finished he cut a long pole for pushing the raft and he used his knife to carve a *crude* paddle, then moved back to the camp before bringing the raft.

   _____

8. And if there was the slightest, tiniest change in Derek, any *indication* at all that he was coming out of it, Brian would call the trip off and hope for the best.

_____

9. He looked into the unconscious man's eyes and saw nothing, just the *glazed* look that was there before.

_____

Part II: Determining the Meaning   Match the vocabulary words to their dictionary definitions.

_____ 1. coma   A. a sign or suggestion
_____ 2. exasperation   B. uncertainties
_____ 3. prying   C. ruled out
_____ 4. doubts   D. glassy-eyed
_____ 5. massive   E. curious looking; snooping
_____ 6. negated   F. roughly made
_____ 7. crude   G. an annoyance
_____ 8. indication   H. enormous
_____ 9. glazed   I. unconsciousness

The River Vocabulary

Chapters 16-19
Part I: Using Prior Knowledge and Context Clues
Below are the sentences in which the vocabulary words appear in the text. Read the sentence. Use any clues you can find in the sentence combined with your prior knowledge, and write what you think the underlined words mean on the lines provided.

1. "Good place to test it," he said. It seemed very *stable* with just Derek on it and Brian carefully eased his knees onto the end by Derek's feet.

   _____

2. Brian leaped forward on the raft, fell on Derek and held him while the raft *lurched*, slid sideways, and settled against the bank, where it stuck in the dirt and brush on the edge of the river.

   _____

3. This time, as they came into a shallow curve and the raft started to move straight, he waited until the raft was close to the shore and used the pole to jam into the bottom and *fend* off.

   _____

4. There were lakes, some large and small, but he was not moving fast enough to have reached any of them yet and that meant the map was not *accurate*.

   _____

5. The thought *stunned* him and he realized how foolish it had been to leave the lake and trust the map.

   _____

6. He wasn't sure if his eyes were being tricked or if it was real, but Derek looked thinner to him and he wondered if getting thinner was a sign of *dehydration*.

   _____

The River Vocabulary

Part II: Determining the Meaning   Match the vocabulary words to their dictionary definitions.

_____ 1. stable   A. exact
_____ 2. lurched   B. sturdy
_____ 3. fend   C. loss of water or moisture
_____ 4. accurate   D. rolled; dipped down
_____ 5. stunned   E. shocked
_____ 6. dehydration   F. to fight against

The River Vocabulary

Chapters 20-Measurements

Part I: Using Prior Knowledge and Context Clues

Below are the sentences in which the vocabulary words appear in the text. Read the sentence. Use any clues you can find in the sentence combined with your prior knowledge, and write what you think the underlined words mean on the lines provided.

1. Twice as fast as he could walk, the raft was fairly *careening* now.

   _____

2. All of this had the effect of making a monstrous *chute* where the water fought and roared to get through, smashing around the rocks in huge sprays of white water.

   _____

3. Derek's body lurched beneath him and dropped back, the raft took the blow, *flexed*, gave, but held together; and Brian started one clear thought: we made it.

   _____

4. As it tipped forward the rear of the raft cut down into the water and came against the *submerged* ledge.

   _____

5. Smashed, *buffeted*, he dragged himself to the side beneath the pressure wave.

   _____

6. He was in the shallows below the rapids, caught up in a small *alcove* in the shoreline.

   _____

7. There was still the sound of water -- although that, too, was *muted*.

   _____

8. Altogether he rounded six shallow bends and still there was no raft, the stupid raft that had hung up on every bend when he was trying to steer it and now _perversely_ held the center of the river somehow.

_____

9. His mother and father _vowed_ never to let him go to the woods again, but relented after some little time when Brian pointed out that of all people who were qualified to be in the wilderness, he certainly was one of them.

_____

10. His mother and father vowed never to let him go to the woods again, but _relented_ after some little time when Brian pointed out that of all people who were qualified to be in the wilderness, he certainly was one of them.

_____

Part II: Determining the Meaning   Match the vocabulary words to their dictionary definitions.

____ 1. careening	A.	covered with water
____ 2. chute	B.	wrongly stubborn
____ 3. flexed	C.	an indentation or small hollow
____ 4. submerged	D.	bent
____ 5. buffeted	E.	eased off
____ 6. alcove	F.	hit; beat
____ 7. muted	G.	promised
____ 8. perversely	H.	rushing headlong
____ 9. vowed	I.	a waterfall; a channel
____ 10. relented	J.	muffled; softened

ANSWER SHEET-PREREADING VOCABULARY WORKSHEETS
The River

Chapters 1-4
1. _____
2. _____
3. _____
4. _____
5. _____
6. _____
7. _____
8. _____
9. _____
10. _____

Chapters 5-7
1. _____
2. _____
3. _____
4. _____

Chapters 8-11
1. _____
2. _____
3. _____
4. _____
5. _____
6. _____
7. _____

Chapters 12-15
1. _____
2. _____
3. _____
4. _____
5. _____
6. _____
7. _____
8. _____
9. _____

Chapters 16-19
1. _____
2. _____
3. _____
4. _____
5. _____
6. _____

Chapters 20- Measurements
1. _____
2. _____
3. _____
4. _____
5. _____
6. _____
7. _____
8. _____
9. _____
10. _____

ANSWER KEY-PREREADING VOCABULARY WORKSHEETS
The River

Chapters 1-4
1. E
2. B
3. H
4. J
5. A
6. I
7. D
8. G
9. C
10. F

Chapters 5-7
1. C
2. A
3. D
4. B

Chapters 8-11
1. C
2. G
3. E
4. B
5. F
6. D
7. A

Chapters 12-15
1. I
2. G
3. E
4. B
5. H
6. C
7. F
8. A
9. D

Chapters 16-19
1. B
2. D
3. F
4. A
5. E
6. C

Chapters 20- Measurements
1. H
2. I
3. D
4. A
5. F
6. C
7. J
8. B
9. G
10. E

DAILY LESSONS

LESSON ONE

Student Objectives
    1. To preview *The River* Unit
    2. To receive books and other related materials (study guides, reading assignment)
    3. To relate prior knowledge to the new material
    4. To become familiar with the vocabulary for Chapters 1-4
    5. To preview the study questions for Chapters 1-4

Activity #1a

    Note to the Teacher: Use this activity if the students have not read *Hatchet*.

    Direct attention to the bulletin board display of wilderness areas. (*The River* does not specifically mention the setting, but it is the northeastern Canadian wilderness, the same as in *Hatchet*.) Ask students to describe what they see. Tell students they will be entering a survival school, and will be sent to a wilderness for a week to learn to survive. Have students form small groups and brainstorm what they would do to survive. Have them make a list of the minimum amount of equipment an supplies they think they would need. Also have them make a list of the possible dangers and problems they could encounter. Each group should record their answers on a piece of paper. Invite students to read their ideas aloud. Collect and save the papers until students have finished reading the novel. Tell students that the boy in the story, Brian Robeson, was stranded in the wilderness with only his hatchet, and survived for 54 days. Now the government wants him to do it again so they can learn from him, and better prepare pilots and others who might actually find themselves in that situation. Take a poll and see how many of the students would repeat the adventure if they were Brian.

Activity #1b

    Note to the Teacher: Use this activity if the students have read *Hatchet*.

    Direct attention to the bulletin board display of wilderness areas. Ask students to name the book they read that had this setting. Invite them to tell as much as they remember about the book *Hatchet*. Have them speculate on what Brian Robeson has been doing since his return to his home in New York. Tell them *The River* takes place about a year after Brian has returned from the wilderness. Some people from a government survival school want him to go to the wilderness again, so they can learn from him how to better train people to survive as he did. Take a poll and see how many of the students would repeat the adventure if they were Brian.

Activity #2

    Distribute the materials students will use in this unit. Explain in detail how students are to use these materials.

    <u>Study Guides</u> Students should preview the study guide questions before each reading assignment to get a feeling for what events and ideas are important in that section. After reading the section, students will (as a class or individually) answer the questions to review the important events and ideas from that section of the book. Students should keep the study guides as study materials.

Reading Assignment Sheet You need to fill in the reading assignment sheet to let students know when their reading has to be completed. You can either write the assignment sheet on a side blackboard or bulletin board and leave it there for students to see each day, or you can "ditto" copies for each student to have. In either case, you should advise students to become very familiar with the reading assignments so they know what is expected of them.

Unit Outline You may find it helpful to distribute copies of the Unit Outline to your students so they can keep track of upcoming lessons and assignments. You may also want to post a copy of the Unit Outline on a bulletin board and cross off each lesson as you complete it.

Extra Activities Center The Unit Resources portion of this unit contains suggestions for a library of related books and articles in your classroom as well as crossword and word search puzzles. Make an extra activities center in your room where you will keep these materials for students to use. Bring the books and articles in from the library and keep several copies of the puzzles on hand. Explain to students that these materials are available for students to use when they finish reading assignments or other class work early.

Books Each school has its own rules and regulations regarding student use of school books. Advise students of the procedures that are normal for your school.

Notebook or Unit Folder You may want the students to keep all of their worksheets, notes, and other papers for the unit together in a binder or notebook. During the first class meeting, tell them how you want them to arrange the folder. Make divider pages for vocabulary worksheets, prereading study guide questions, review activities, notes, and tests. You may want to give a grade for accuracy in keeping the folder.

Activity #3

Do a group KWL Sheet with the students (form included.) Some students will know something about Gary Paulsen or his books and will have information to share. Put this information in the K column (What I Know.) Ask students what they want to find out from reading the book and record this in the W column (What I Want to Find Out.) Keep the sheet and refer back to it after reading the book. Complete the L column (What I Learned) at that time.

Activity #4

Work through the prereading vocabulary worksheet for Chapters 1-4 with the students. Tell them they will have a sheet like this to complete before reading each section of the book.

Activity #5

Show students how to preview the study questions for Chapters 1-4 of *The River*. Encourage students to predict what they think answers might be, to write down their predictions, and to compare these with their answers after reading the chapters.

KWL *The River*

Directions: Before reading, think about what you already know about Gary Paulsen and/or *The River*. Write the information in the K column. Think about what you would like to find out from reading the book. Write your questions in the W column. After you have read the book, use the L column to write the answers to your questions from the W column, and anything else you remember from the book.

K **What I Know**	**W** **What I Want to Find Out**	**L** **What I Learned**

LESSON TWO

Student Objectives
1. To understand plot development and record plot information on a chart
2. To read Chapters 1-4

Activity #1: Minilesson: Plot

Tell students they will be discussing and mapping the plot of the novel. **Plot** refers to the events in the novel. It tells what the characters do, what happens to them, and how things happen. The plot is usually told in sequence. Plot structure is usually either conflict-resolution or goal-achievement. The main types of conflicts are character vs. character, character vs. nature, character vs. self, and character vs. society. (If you have used the study guide for *Hatchet*, refer to the lessons on conflict now.) In a goal-achievement plot structure, the main character sets a goal and the plot progresses until the goal is achieved or not achieved. *The River* has a combination of conflict-resolution and goal-achievement. The **climax** is the highest point of action or suspense. The reader does not yet know the outcome. The **resolution** or **outcome** occurs at the end of the story.

Use a Plot Diagram to help students identify the main conflicts and events in the novel. Encourage students to identify conflicts as they read. After reading Chapters 1-4, complete the beginning of a of the plot diagram with students.

Activity #2

You may want to read Chapter 1 aloud to the students to set the mood for the novel. Invite willing students to read Chapters 2-4 aloud to the rest of the class.

Activity #3

Tell students they will discuss the study questions during the next class meeting. If time permits, allow them to begin working on the questions in class.

LESSON THREE

Student Objectives
    1. To review the main ideas and themes in Chapters 1-4
    2. To become familiar with the vocabulary for Chapters 5-7
    3. To preview the study questions for Chapters 5-7
    4. To read Chapters 5-7

Activity #1

    Discuss the answers to the Study Guide questions for Chapters 1-4 in detail. Write the answers on the board or overhead projector so students can have the correct answers for study purposes. Encourage students to take notes. If the students own their books, encourage them to use highlighter pens to mark important passages and the answers to the study guide questions.

    Note: It is a good practice in public speaking and leadership skills for individuals students to take charge of leading the discussion of the study questions. Perhaps a different student could go to the front of the class and lead the discussion each day that the study questions are discussed during this unit. Of course, the teacher should guide the discussion when appropriate and be sure to fill in any gaps the students leave.

Activity #2

    Give students about ten or fifteen minutes to do the prereading vocabulary work and preview the study questions for Chapters 5-7.

Activity #3

    Give the students the rest of the class period to read silently. Tell them they should have the reading completed for the next class meeting.

LESSON FOUR

Student Objectives
1. To identify the examples of flashback and foreshadowing in the novel so far
2. To answer the study questions for Chapters 5-7

Activity #1 Minilesson: Flashback and Foreshadowing

Flashback is a literary device in which the author inserts a previous event into the current event or scene in the story. It is used to give the reader a better understanding of the character's behavior or motivation in the present. A flashback may take place as a dream or as a memory. Paulsen uses several instances of flashback throughout the novel to explain events from Brian's first time in the wilderness.

You may want to show a visual illustration of how a flashback is used. A clip from a television show or movie that uses a flashback will be effective. You could also draw a picture of Brian in the cockpit of the plane with a thought balloon above his head. He could be visualizing the plane crash from his first time in the wilderness.

Foreshadowing uses words and phrases that give readers clues about events that have not yet occurred.

Read the following excerpts from the novel and have students identify them as foreshadowing or flashback:

1) Chapter 1, flashback: For months after his return home, Brian had been followed by the press. Even after the television special--a camera crew went back with him to the lake and he showed them how he'd lived--they stayed after him. (This continues for a few more paragraphs.)
2) Chapter 2, flashback: Brian had a mental picture of the porcupine coming into his shelter in the dark, throwing the hatchet and hitting the rock embedded in the wall and getting sparks.
3) Chapter 6, foreshadowing: Later, when everything changed and he did not think there was hope, that statement was all that kept Brian going.

Divide a bulletin board into two sections labeled Flashback and Foreshadowing. Have several index cards available. Invite students to copy the examples of flashback and foreshadowing from the text onto the cards and display them on the bulletin board. Suggest that they illustrate the examples.

Activity #2

Have students work individually or in pairs to answer the study questions. Then go over the answers with the students.

LESSON 5

Student Objective
    1. To become familiar with the non-fiction assignment
    2. To practice writing to inform
    3. To learn to do library research

Activity #1

    Distribute copies of the Nonfiction Assignment sheet and go over it in detail with the students. Explain to students that they each are to read at least one nonfiction piece, write a report about it, and fill in the Nonfiction Assignment Sheet. They will also present their information to the class in the form of an oral report during Lesson 20. The nonfiction piece could be a book, a magazine article, or information from an encyclopedia or the Internet. You could also consider letting students watch an educational television show or video, such as a documentary. Give them the due date for the assignment (Lesson 8 for the writing assignment, Lesson 20 for the Nonfiction Assignment Sheet and Oral Report.)

    Encourage students to research topics that are related to the theme of the novel. Some suggestions are: wilderness survival, physical characteristics of the Canadian wilderness; animals of the Canadian wilderness; lightning and its effects; shock and comas brought on by lightning, trading posts, fur trade, small aircraft; the history of hand tools; survival programs such as Outward Bound; psychology, the history of fire, edible plants in the wild, and the effects of divorce on children.

Activity #2

    Distribute copies of Writing Assignment #1. Go over the assignment in detail with the students. Tell them they will have the remainder of the class period to begin working on the assignment. Give the due date for the completed assignment. It should be a few days before the writing conferences, which are scheduled for Lesson 10.

Activity #3

    Distribute copies of the Writing Evaluation Form (included with this Unit Plan.) Explain to students that during Lesson Ten you will be holding individual writing conferences about this writing assignment. Make sure students are familiar with the criteria on the Writing Evaluation Form.

Follow Up: After you have graded the assignments, have a writing conference with each student. This Unit Plan schedules one in Lesson 10. After the writing conference, allow students to revise their papers using your suggestions to complete the revisions. Grade the revisions on an A-C-E scale: A = all revisions well done; C = some revisions made; E = few or no revisions made. This will speed your grading time and still give some credit for the students' efforts.

Activity #4

    Take the students to the library to work, if possible.

WRITING ASSIGNMENT #1 *The River*
Writing to Inform

PROMPT

You are reading about Brian Robeson, who previously survived for 54 days alone in the Canadian wilderness. All he had with him was a small hatchet. Now, the government has asked him to go into the wilderness with one of their psychologists so they can learn how he survived.

When he returned, Brian did some research on his surroundings. He found out the kinds of animals and plants that had been near the lake. He also read about the history of fire. Your assignment is to find out more about one of the nonfiction topics mentioned in the novel. You will write a short report about your findings.

PREWRITING

Choose a topic or topics that interest you. Go to the library and find as many sources as you can on the topic. Look for encyclopedias, books, magazine articles, videos, and Internet sources. You may want to interview an expert on the topic of your choice.

Think of questions you have about your topic. Write each one on a separate index card. Then read to find the answers, and write them on the cards. Also take notes on interesting and important facts, even if you did not have questions about them. Put each fact on a separate card. Make sure to cite your references. That means to write down the source and the page number for each one.

Arrange your note card in the order you want to use for your paper.

DRAFTING

Introduce your topic in the first paragraph. Tell why you chose it, and give a preview of what the rest of the paper will be about. Then write several paragraphs about the topic. Each paragraph should have a main idea and supporting details. Your last paragraph should summarize the information in the report.

PEER CONFERENCE/REVISING

When you finish the rough draft, ask another student to look at it. You may want to give the student your note cards so he/she can double check for you and see that you have included all of the information. After reading, he or she should tell you what he/she liked best about your report, which parts were difficult to understand or needed more information, and ways in which your work could be improved. Reread your report considering your critic's comments and make the corrections you think are necessary.

PROOFREADING/EDITING

Do a final proofreading of your report, double-checking your grammar, spelling, organization, and the clarity of your ideas.

NONFICTION ASSIGNMENT SHEET *The River*
(To be completed after reading the required nonfiction article)

Name _____ Date _____ Class _____

Title of Nonfiction Read _____

Written By _____ Publication Date _____

I. Factual Summary: Write a short summary of the piece you read.

II. Vocabulary:
    1. Which vocabulary words were difficult?

    2. What did you do to help yourself understand the words?

III. Interpretation: What was the main point the author wanted you to get from reading his/her work?

IV. Criticism:
    1. Which points of the piece did you agree with or find easy to believe? Why?

    2. With which points of the piece did you disagree or find difficult to believe? Why?

V. Personal Response:
    1. What do you think about this piece?

    2. How does this piece help you better understand the novel *The River*?

WRITING EVALUATION FORM *The River*
Writing Assignment # 1 Writing to Inform

Name _____ Date _____ Class _____

Circle One For Each Item:

Composition	excellent	good	fair	poor
Style	excellent	good	fair	poor
Grammar	excellent	good	fair	poor (errors noted)
Spelling	excellent	good	fair	poor (errors noted)
Punctuation	excellent	good	fair	poor (errors noted)
Legibility	excellent	good	fair	poor (errors noted)

Strengths:

Weaknesses:

Comments/Suggestions:

LESSON 6

Student Objectives
1. To become familiar with the vocabulary for Chapters 8-11
2. To preview the study questions for Chapters 8-11
3. To read Chapters 8-11 orally for evaluation
4. To practice correct intonation and expression in oral reading

Activity #1
Give students about fifteen minutes to go over the vocabulary and study guide questions for Chapters 8-11.

Activity #2
Tell students their oral reading ability will be evaluated. Show them copies of the Oral Reading Evaluation Form and discuss it. Model correct intonation and expression by reading the first few paragraphs of Chapter 8 aloud.

Call on individual students to read a few paragraphs aloud. Encourage the other students to follow along silently in their books. If you have a student who is unwilling or unable to read in front of the group make arrangements to do his or her evaluation privately at another time.

LESSON SEVEN

Student Objectives
1. To discuss the main ideas and events in Chapters 8-11
2. To become familiar with the vocabulary for Chapters 12-15
3. To preview the study questions for Chapters 12-15
4. To read Chapters 12-15

Activity #1
Divide the class into seven groups, one for each question. have each group find the answer to one of the questions, and present it to the class. They must have the page reference from the book, and be able to either read the passages aloud, or dramatize the events discussed in the question and answer.

Activity #2
Give students about ten minutes to complete the prereading vocabulary worksheet. Have students also look at the study questions and make predictions about the answers.

Activity #4
Tell students they will be having a quiz on Chapters 1-11 during the next class period. Give them the rest of the period to study quietly or read Chapters 12-15. Tell them that the questions for Chapters 12-15 will be due during Lesson 9.

ORAL READING EVALUATION *The River*

Name_____ Class_____ Date _____

SKILL	EXCELLENT	GOOD	AVERAGE	FAIR	POOR
Fluency	5	4	3	2	1
Clarity	5	4	3	2	1
Audibility	5	4	3	2	1
Pronunciation	5	4	3	2	1
	5	4	3	2	1
	5	4	3	2	1

Total _____ Grade _____

Comments:

LESSON EIGHT

Student Objectives

    1. To take a quiz on Chapters 1-11
    2. To practice writing to persuade

Activity #1

    Quiz--distribute quizzes (multiple choice study questions for Chapters 1-11) and give students about fifteen minutes to complete them. Collect the papers for scoring and recording the grades.

Activity #2

    Introduce Writing Assignment #2. Give the students the rest of the period to work on it.

Publishing Suggestions

Display the completed posters on a bulletin board or empty wall.
Let students videotape their commercials and show them to the class.
Have students give live presentations of their ads to the class.

Option

You may want to let students work with a partner or a small group for this assignment. If so, make sure they understand that they will all receive the same grade.

LESSON NINE

Student Objectives

    1. To review the main ideas and themes in Chapters 12-15
    2. To discuss the progression of the plot
    3. To add information to the plot diagram

Activity # 1

    Arrange students in small groups and let each group choose a question and answer to dramatize. Spend about twenty minutes (about three minutes per question) watching and discussing the dramatizations.

Activity #2 Minilesson: Plot

    Refer to the Plot Diagram the students started in Lesson Two. Discuss the conflicts that have occurred in the story so far, and the character's reactions to them. Have students add the information to their diagrams. Remind students that the climax is the most intense or deeply felt point of the story. The reader will respond to it emotionally. The climax follows some type of crisis in the plot, and involves a turning point in the action of the story. Suggest that they keep this information in mind as they read the rest of the novel, and look for the climax. Tell them they will complete the plot diagram during Lesson Thirteen.

WRITING ASSIGNMENT #2 *The River*
Writing to Persuade

PROMPT

    When Brian first returned home from his time in the wilderness, the media paid a lot of attention to him. One man wanted to use Brian's face on a T-shirt. Another company wanted to design a line of Brian Robeson Survival Jeans. You are a product designer for a company. Your job is to think of a product related to Brian's time in the wilderness. Then you must create an advertisement to sell your product to the public.

PREWRITING

    You can design any kind of product you want, as long as it relates somehow to survival and /or living in the wilderness. Your product can be clothing, food, or supplies. While the people who will buy your product may not actually use it in the wilderness, it should still appeal to them because of the association with being rugged and being able to survive. You will draw or make a sample of your product, so keep it simple. First, think of a product. You may want to look through camping catalogs or magazines to get some ideas. Next, make a list of reasons why someone should buy your product. Arrange the list putting your best or strongest reasons first. Then, think of a jingle or slogan to advertise your product. This should be a few words or a short sentence that will grab the reader or viewer's attention. It should make them remember your product. For example, one cereal advertises itself as "The breakfast of champions."

DRAFTING

    Make a sketch or a model of your product. If possible, make it the right size. If your product is very large, use graph paper and draw a scale model. Work on the jingle or slogan next. Try several versions until you find one that sounds appealing. Say it out loud several times. Is it something you would remember? Next, design a poster to advertise the product. Use colors that will attract the viewer. Put a drawing of the product on the poster. If your model is small enough, attach it to the poster. Then add the jingle. Use lettering that is neat, large, and easy to read.

PEER CONFERENCING/REVISING

    When you finish the rough draft, ask another student to look at it. After reading, he or she should tell you what he/she liked best about your advertisement, which parts were difficult to understand or needed more information, and ways in which your work could be improved. Reread your advertisement considering your critic's comments and make the corrections you think are necessary.

PROOFREADING/EDITING

    Do a final proofreading of your advertisement, double-checking your grammar, spelling, organization, and the clarity of your ideas.

LESSON TEN

Student Objectives
    1. To participate in a writing conference with the teacher
    2. To revise Writing Assignment #1

Activity #1
    Choose a quiet corner of the room and hold the individual writing conferences.

Activity #2
    Allow the rest of the class period for students to work on the revising Writing Assignment #1, or catching up on other reading work.

LESSON ELEVEN

Student Objectives
    1. To become familiar with the vocabulary for Chapters 16-19
    2. To preview the study questions for Chapters 16-19
    3. To read Chapters 16-19

Activity #1
    Give students ten or fifteen minutes to compete the prereading vocabulary work. Then pass out drawing paper, and have each student illustrate one of the words. Hold each illustration up to the class and have them identify the word being illustrated.

Activity #2
    Put the prereading questions for Chapters 16-17 on the board or on an overhead transparency. Ask students to choose one question they would like to answer after reading. Group the students according to their choices. Have each group prepare the answer to their question after they have read the text. They may give the answer by reading the information from the text, summarizing it, or dramatizing the event.

Activity #3
    Let students begin reading the chapters in the time remaining. Remind them that the reading, and their answer to the question they chose, must be completed before the next class meeting.

LESSON TWELVE

Student Objectives
1. To review the main ideas and events in Chapters 16-19
2. To identify examples of simile in the novel

Activity #1

Have the groups formed during Lesson Eleven give their answers to the study guide questions.

Activity #2 Minilesson: Simile

Write the following sentences on the board:

Brian was as hungry as a horse when he first got home from the wilderness.

For a while, the news media chased after him and he felt like a movie star.

Tell students these are examples of similes. Similes are comparisons where the writer tells the reader that two things are alike. Similes use the words **like** or **as**. Authors use similes to create vivid descriptions of characters, settings, and events. Readers need to recognize similes to appreciate the writer's style and understand the story.

Have students find the examples of simile in the chapters they have read so far and record them on the Simile Chart. Encourage them to keep the chart and record more examples as they read.

Chapter 5:	There was absolutely no wind, and the water was as smooth as a mirror.
	He's as excited as a kid.
Chapter 6:	. . . and in a small time he was jerking up and down like a yo-yo.
	. . . the night temperature began to drop and it was as if a switch went off.
Chapter 7:	Brian felt like he'd been hit by a truck.
	"Kind of like a drowned rat."
	I sound like a catalog, he thought, *like I'm reading a telephone book.*
Chapter 8:	Derek looked at the depression. "It looks like a hole. . . . "
Chapter 10:	Like a camera taking pictures by a strobe light, things would seem frozen in time. . .
Chapter 15:	. . . and dropped trees fallen across each other so thickly that it looked like giants had started to play pick-up-sticks and walked away before finishing the game.
Chapter 16:	Again, it was like moving dead weight.
Chapter 18:	"It's like paddling a brushpile," he said to Derek.
Chapter 21:	The current roared past the rock and took him like a chip, sucking him downstream.

SIMILE CHART *The River*

SIMILE	OBJECTS BEING COMPARED	MEANING
the water was as smooth as a mirror (ch. 5)	water and a mirror	the water was flat and smooth

LESSON THIRTEEN

Student Objectives
1. To become familiar with the vocabulary for Chapters 20-Measurements
2. To make a prediction about the outcome of the story
3. To read Chapters 20-Measurements
4. To discuss the main ideas and events in Chapters 20-Measurements
5. To complete the plot diagram

Activity #1
Give students about fifteen minutes to complete the prereading vocabulary worksheet.

Activity #2
Tell students they will not be previewing the study guide questions for this section of the novel. Instead, have them write down the way they think the story will end.

Activity #3
Have students read Chapters 20-Measurements silently independently, or quietly read aloud with a partner.

Activity #4
Give each student four 1"x2" strips of colored paper or index cards--one blue, one yellow, one green, one pink. Have them put a large letter A on the blue paper, B on the yellow, C on the green, and D on the pink. Distribute copies of the Multiple Choice/Quiz questions for Chapters 20-Measurements. Ask students to read the first question and hold up the colored paper for the correct answer. Then have them mark the correct answer on their worksheets.

Activity #5
Work with students to complete the plot diagram.

LESSON FOURTEEN

Student Objective
    To discuss *The River at* the interpretive and critical levels

Activity #1
    Choose the questions from the Extra Writing Assignments/Discussion Questions which seem most appropriate for your students. A class discussion of these questions is most effective if students have been given the opportunity to formulate answers to the questions prior to the discussion. To this end, you may either have all the students formulate answers to all the questions, divide the class into groups and assign one or more questions to each group, or you could assign one question to each student in your class. The option you choose will make a difference in the amount of class time needed for this activity.

Activity #2
    After students have had ample time to formulate answers to the questions, begin your class discussion of the questions and the ideas presented by the questions. Be sure students take notes during the discussion so they have information to study for the unit test.

EXTRA WRITING ASSIGNMENT/DISCUSSION QUESTIONS
The River

<u>Interpretation</u>

1. From what point of view is the story written? How does this affect our understanding of the story?

2. What are the main conflicts in the story? Are they resolved? If so, how? If not, why not?

3. What is the setting? How important is the setting to the story? Why?

4. Write a character sketch of Brian Robeson.

5. Why did Brian feel that he had to be evasive, to hold back?

6. Why did Brian's mother put the hatchet in the china closet?

7. Describe Brian's relationship with his mother

8. Why do you think he liked to cook after he returned from his time in the wilderness?

9. Why did Brian feel he had to "revert" and "rectify" when he returned from the wilderness?

10. Why did Brian's parents want him to go to a counselor?

11. Why didn't the counselor seem to help Brian?

12. Why did Brian think the easy time was all wrong? What does this tell about his character?

13. How did Brian's first experience in the wilderness make his second one easier?

14. Why was Brian planning to just wait for Derek to come to? Why didn't he think of any other course of action?

15. What was the greatest danger that Brian faced? Why do you think so?

Extra Discussion Questions *The River*

Critical
16. Is the story believable? Why or why not?

17. How did Brian change over the course of the novel? Were these changes for the better?

18. Was the character of Brian believable?

19. Was the character of Derek believable?

20. Paulsen often used vivid language to describe a scene or event. Give an example of his use of vivid language that you found most effective. Tell why it was effective.

21. What was the overall mood of the story? Give examples to support your answer.

22. Identify a few of the examples of simile and discuss their contribution to the novel.

23. Explain the statement: "He became something other than himself that afternoon."

24. Give examples of foreshadowing in the novel. Were they effective?

25. Brian has already shown that he can survive in the wilderness. How does Gary Paulsen hold the reader's interest as Brian goes into the wilderness for the second time?

26. Describe Gary Paulsen's writing style. How does it shape the reader's reaction to the story?

27. Brian compares his raft to something out of *Huckleberry Finn*. Is this a good comparison?

Personal Response
28. Did you enjoy reading *The River?* Why or why not?

29. Is *The River* a good title for the book? Why or why not? If not, what title would you suggest?

30. Brian didn't take the hatchet because he said most people in his situation would not have one. Do you think he had any other reasons for not taking it?

31. According to Derek, it was psychologically wrong for survival course participants to have tents and insect repellent to "take the edge off." Do you agree or disagree? Why?

Extra Discussion Questions *The River*

32. How do you think Brian felt when he saw that Derek was injured and the radio was broken?

33. Brian says that many people told him they would like to try to survive in the wilderness the way he did. Would you like to? Why or why not?

34. What do you think the government will do about survival training?

35. The counselor thought Brian was mentally injured from the first wilderness experience. Brian thought the truth was the opposite, that he was more than he had been before. Which opinion do you agree with? Why?

36. Have you read any of Gary Paulsen's other books? Which ones? Which did you like best? Why?

37. Will you read more of Gary Paulsen's books? Why or why not?

38. Before you read the story, did you think it would be possible to survive in the wilderness alone? What do you think after reading the story?

39. Did Brian's experiences change the way you look at yourself? How?

40. Brian and Derek thought the beginning of their trip lacked tension. Do you agree or disagree? Why?

41. Would you recommend this book to another student? Why or why not?

QUOTATIONS *The River*
Discuss the significance of the following quotations.

1. "Well, to make it short, we want you to do it again."

2. "But that's crazy. It was . . . rough. I mean, I almost died and it was just luck that I made it out."

3. "No, not luck. You had something more going for you besides luck."

4. "It wasn't like you think. It wasn't a camping trip. I lost weight, but more than that, I didn't come back the same."

5. "No. You don't understand. I truly discovered fire--the way some man or woman did it thousands of years ago. . . . I truly and honestly discovered fire. It was a real thing, a very great thing."

6. To have dishes, he thought, just to have dishes and pots and pans and a stove to cook the food--it still marveled him.

7. "I don't think you have the slightest idea of what you're asking. You must realize that for the time Brian was gone we thought he was dead. Dead. We were told by experts that he couldn't possibly still be alive and then we got him back. Back from the dead. And now you're asking me--his mother--to send him back out there?"

8. "I have to do it."

9. "I don't mean hunger like you're thinking of it," he had told her. "Not just when you miss a meal and feel like eating a little bit. Or even if you go a day without eating. I mean where you don't think you're ever going to eat again--don't know if there will ever be more food. An end to food. Where you won't eat and you won't eat and then you still won't eat and finally you *still* won't eat and even when you die and are gone, even then there won't be any food. *That* kind of hunger."

10. "I was just . . . looking at things. Seeing them."

11. "That's it exactly. We have trouble. That's what this is all about. You want to learn, but if you have all that backup, it's just me or games. It's not real. You wouldn't have that if the situation were real, would you?"

Quotations *The River*

12. "You must settle. In your mind. There are some fights you can't win, and I think this must be one of them. It will get worse and worse until after the middle of the night, when the coolness comes and the mosquitoes will stop. Or at least a lot of them will."

13. "I had forgotten," Brian said. "I had dreams after I got out the last time. Not all nightmares, but dreams. I would dream of this, of how pretty it was, how it could stop your breath with it, and then I would wake up in my room with the traffic sounds and the streetlights outside and I would feel bad--miss it. I would miss this."

14. "You're so . . . so quiet. I mean, I see you looking at things and thinking, but I don't know what you're thinking about or what you're working out. I have to know all this to write about it, to tell people what to do."

15. "Food is everything. . . Just that. Out here, in nature, in the world, food is everything. All the other parts of what we are, what everything is, don't matter without food. I read somewhere that all of what man is, everything man has always been or will be, all the thoughts and dreams and sex and hate and every little and big thing is dependent on six inches of topsoil and rain when you need it to make a crop grow--food."

16. "That's *all* I did--think of food. You watch other animals, birds, fish, even down to ants--they spend all their time working at food. Getting something to eat. That's what nature is, really--getting food. And when you're out here, having to live, you look for food. Food first. Food. *Food.*"

17. "You move and you watch and you work hard and you just keep doing that until luck comes. If it's bad luck you ride it out and if it comes the other way and you have good luck you're ready for it."

18. "No more mosquitoes."

19. "You can't have too much wood. Ever. And you should always have dried wood stashed back in some safe place, along with tinder."

Quotations *The River*

20. "Fire. It's so . . . so alive. Such an important thing to us. Back there in the world we don't know that. But when I got home last time I tried to read abut what it was like, you know, before we got everything we have now. In colonial times they kept people awake just to watch the fires, and in ancient times the most important person in the tribe was called the fire watcher."

21. "All this. We're so . . . so ready. So calm. It doesn't work, somehow. None of it works."

22. Then he was leaning forward and his hand was out, reaching for his briefcase and radio next to the bed, one finger out, his face concentrating; and Brian thought, no, don't reach, stay low,; and he might have yelled it , screamed it, but it didn't matter. No sound could be loud enough to get over the thunder.

23. *Let's reason it out,* he thought, his mind as blurred as his vision. Reason it all out.

24. "Katie One, this is Katie Two, over."

25. In the night, next to Derek, he tried to will him awake. *Snap awake now and ask how long you've been sleeping. Now. And we'll laugh and talk about how close the lightning came.*

26. *Listen to me*, he thought. *If I were talking out loud, I'd be whining. Derek gets hit and I act like I'm the one getting messed up.*

27. *I can't do this,* he thought. *I can't do this alone. I just can't.*

28. "Arrived ," he read aloud. Brian demanded that we leave all the gear in the plane or it would ruin the whole experiment. . . . I admire his ethics."

29. "Isn't that a funny name," his mother had said, and Derek had laughed.

30. "Here it is--I could leave you and try to follow the river out and bring help back. . . . I can't leave you."

31. "Lots of people carry a knife of some kind," Derek had said. "But how many have a hatchet on their belt?"

32. It's like I hired them, Brian thought, looking at all the fallen poplars--just to cut them down for me.

Quotations *The River*

33. Like something out of *Huckleberry Finn*, he thought.

34. "We go."

35. "Derek, I don't know if you can hear me. I'm going to tell you anyway. We're going to take this raft down the river that leads from the lake. It's just under a hundred miles to the trading post. The thing is, we can't stay here because . . . well, it just wouldn't work. And the radio was blown by the same lightning that hit you. So we can't call for help. So we have to do this, we have to do this. . . . "

36. Big storm. Derek hit by lightning and in a coma. Trying to raft river down to Brannock's Trading Post 100 miles south. Come quick. Brian Robeson.

37. "It's all right," she said. "You can let go now--it's all right."

38. *So use thought, use logic. Use it. Think.*

39. "It's like paddling a brushpile," he said to Derek. "Nothing seems to move."

40. "All the way," he mumbled, reaching with the paddle again. "We go all the way together."

41. "We're moving. . . We're moving along now. . . We're hauling. . . . "

42. "I'll have to swim."

43. It was as if everything came loose in Brian at the same time. His body, his mind, his soul were all exhausted and he fell across Derek, asleep or unconscious, fell with his legs still in the water. "Derek."

44. "Help. Help me."

45. "Next time," he read aloud, "it won't be so hard to paddle. Thanks."

LESSON FIFTEEN

<u>Student Objective</u>
　　To write to express a personal opinion

<u>Activity #1</u>
　　Engage students in a discussion of Brian's comments early in the novel about not coming back the same from his first time in the wilderness. Encourage them to think about an experience they had that somehow changed them. Invite students to share their experiences.

<u>Activity #2</u>
　　Distribute copies of Writing Assignment #3 and go over it in detail with the class.

<u>Activity #3</u>
　　Give students the rest of the class period to work on the assignment. If you are giving them longer than the one class period to complete it, assign the due date.

WRITING ASSIGNMENT #3 *The River*
Writing to Express a personal Opinion

PROMPT

In Chapter 2 of *The River,* Brian thinks about the ways that his time in the wilderness changed him. While you have probably not been stranded alone as Brian was, you have most likely had one or more experiences that changed you in some way. Your assignment is to think about that experience and how it changed you. You will write about the experiences and changes in the form of a poem.

PREWRITING

Spend some time thinking about the way you are now. You may want to write a description of yourself, physically and mentally, as you are now. Next, think back a few months or years. What were you like then? If you have journals or diaries, reread them to get a picture of the way you used to be. Ask yourself how you are different now, and what experiences influenced the changes in you.

DRAFTING

Write your poem using the following formula. (A formula is a certain way to do something.) The formula for this poem is:

    I used to _____
    But now _____ .

In this type of poem, you compare and contrast yourself. You can use as may comparisons as you want. Your poem can have as many verses as you want. The lines in this poem do not have to rhyme.

    Here is an example of a poem:
        I used to be a chatterbox,
        But now I am as quiet as a mouse.

        In kindergarten, I used to cry when my mom left me,
        But now I wave good bye and jump on the bus.

PROMPT

When you finish the rough draft, ask another student to look at it. After reading, he or she should tell you what he/she liked best about your poem, which parts were difficult to understand or needed more information, and ways in which your work could be improved. Reread your poem considering your critic's comments and make the corrections you think are necessary.

PROOFREADING/EDITING

Do a final proofreading of your poem, double-checking your grammar, spelling, organization, and the clarity of your ideas.

LESSON SIXTEEN

Student Objectives
1. To extend the story by means of a project
2. To work cooperatively in a group

Activity #1
Allow students to choose one of the following projects. Give them the class period to complete it. If students need more time, you can assign the project as homework or add another day onto the unit plan.

PROJECT IDEAS

1. Draw a book jacket that summarizes the story.

2. Write a critique of the book.

3. Make a timeline showing the important events from the story.

4. Make a diorama showing one of the scenes from the book.

5. Make a clay or wooden model of the raft.

6. Make puppets and write a puppet show to illustrate one scene from the story.

7. Write a radio or television commercial to advertise the book.

8. Design a poster to advertise the book.

9. Write a different ending to the story.

10. Make a comic book version of the story to share with younger readers.

11. Make a mobile showing the main character, secondary characters and setting.

13. Create a "Missing Person" poster describing Brian and Derek.

14. Create a poster showing wilderness survival techniques.

15. Make a collage based on scenes from the book.

16. Create a journal entry from Derek's notebook.

17. Write a short wilderness survival manual based on Brian's experiences and the things he told Derek.

18. Write a poem about the book, or in response to it.

19. Write a movie script based on the book.

20. Write Derek's final report to the government about his trip. Include recommendations for the survival school course.

LESSON SEVENTEEN

Student Objective
To review all of the vocabulary work done in this unit

VOCABULARY REVIEW ACTIVITIES

1. Divide your class into two teams and have an old-fashioned spelling or definition bee.

2. Give individuals or groups of students a *The River* Vocabulary Word Search Puzzle. The person (group) to find all of the vocabulary words in the puzzle first wins.

3. Give students a *The River* Vocabulary Word Search Puzzle without the word list. The person or group to find the most vocabulary words in the puzzle wins.

4. Put a *The River* Vocabulary Crossword Puzzle onto a transparency on the overhead projector and do the puzzle together as a class.

5. Give students a *The River* Vocabulary Matching Worksheet to do.

6. Use words from the word jumble page and have students spell them correctly.

7. Have students write a story in which they correctly use as many vocabulary words as possible. Have students read their compositions orally. Post the most original compositions on your bulletin board.

8. Have students work in teams and play charades with the vocabulary words.

9. Select a word of the day and encourage students to use it correctly in their writing and speaking vocabulary.

10. Have a contest to see which students can find the most vocabulary words used in other sources. You may want to have a bulletin board available so the students can write down their word, the sentence it was used in, and the source.

11. Assign a word to each student, or let them choose a word. Have them look up the origin of the word, the part of speech, definition, a synonym, and an antonym. Then have them write a sentence using the word. Have students present their information orally to the class, or have them design a word map on paper and display the papers.

LESSON EIGHTEEN

Objective
To review the main ideas presented in *The River*

Activity #1
Choose one of the review games/activities included in the packet and spend your class period as outlined there.

Activity #2
Remind students of the date for the Unit Test. Stress the review of the Study Guides and their class notes as a last minute, brush-up review for homework.

REVIEW GAMES / ACTIVITIES

1. Ask the class to make up a unit test for *The River*. The test should have 4 sections: multiple choice, true/false, short answer and essay. Students may use 1/2 period to make the test, including a separate answer sheet, and then swap papers and use the other 1/2 class period to take a test a classmate has devised. (open book)

2. Take 1/2 period for students to make up true and false questions (including the answers). Collect the papers and divide the class into two teams. Draw a big tic-tac-toe board on the chalk board. Make one team X and one team O. Ask questions to each side, giving each student one turn. If the question is answered correctly, that student's team's letter (X or O) is placed in the box. If the answer is incorrect, no mark is placed in the box. The object is to get three marks in a row like tic-tac-toe. You may want to keep track of the number of games won for each team.

3. Take 1/2 period for students to make up questions (true/false and short answer). Collect the questions. Divide the class into two teams. You'll alternate asking questions to individual members of teams A & B (like in a spelling bee). The question keeps going from A to B until it is correctly answered, then a new question is asked. A correct answer does not allow the team to get another question. Correct answers are +2 points; incorrect answers are -1 point.

4. Allow students time to quiz each other (in pairs) from their study guides and class notes.

5. Give students a *The River* crossword puzzle to complete.

REVIEW GAMES / ACTIVITIES Continued

6. Divide your class into two teams. Use *The River* crossword words with their letters jumbled as a word list. Student 1 from Team A faces off against Student 1 from Team B. You write the first jumbled word on the board. The first student (1A or 1B) to unscramble the word wins the chance for his/her team to score points. If 1A wins the jumble, go to student 2A and give him/her a clue. He/she must give you the correct word which matches that clue. If he/she does, Team A scores a point, and you give student 3A a clue for which you expect another correct response. Continue giving Team A clues until some team member makes an incorrect response. An incorrect response sends the game back to the jumbled-word face off, this time with students 2A and 2B. Instead of repeating giving clues to the first few students of each team, continue with the student after the one who gave the last incorrect response on the team.

7. Take on the persona of "The Answer Person." Allow students to ask any question about the book. Answer the questions, or tell students where to look in the book to find the answer.

8. Students may enjoy playing charades with events from the story. Select a student to start. Give him/her a card with a scene or event from the story. Allow the players to use their books to find the scene being described. The first person to guess each charade performs the next one.

9. Play a categories-type quiz game. (A master is included in this Unit Plan). Make an overhead transparency of the categories form. Divide the class into teams of three or four players each. Have each team Choose a recorder and a banker. Choose a team to go first. That team will choose a category and point amount. Ask the question to the entire class.(Use the Study Guide Quiz and Vocabulary questions.) Give the teams one minute to discuss the answer and write it down. Walk around the room and check the answers. Each team that answers correctly receives the points. (Incorrect answers are not penalized; they just don't receive any points). Cross out that square on the playing board. Play continues until all squares have been used. The winning team is the one with the most points. You can assign bonus points to any square or squares you choose.

10. Have individual students draw scenes from the book. Display the scenes and have the rest of the class look in their books to find the chapter or section that is being depicted. The first student to find the correct scene then displays his or her picture. When the game is over, collect the pictures and put them in a binder for students to look at during their free time.

NOTE: If students do not need the extra review, omit this lesson and go on to the test.

QUIZ GAME
The River

Chapters 1-4	Chapters 5-7	Chapters 8-11	Chapters 12-15	Chapters 16-19	Chapters 20-Measurements
100	100	100	100	100	100
200	200	200	200	200	200
300	300	300	300	300	300
400	400	400	400	400	400
500	500	500	500	500	500

LESSON NINETEEN

Objective
   To test the students' understanding of the main ideas and themes in *The River*

Activity #1
   Distribute *The River Unit* Tests. Go over the instructions in detail and allow the students the entire class period to complete the exam.

Activity #2
   Collect all test papers and assigned books prior to the end of the class period.

NOTES ABOUT THE UNIT TESTS IN THIS UNIT:

There are 5 different unit tests which follow.

There are two short answer tests which are based primarily on facts from the novel. The answer key for short answer unit test 1 follows the student test. The answer key for short answer test 2 follows the student short answer unit test 2.

There is one advanced short answer unit test. It is based on the extra discussion questions. Use the matching key for short answer unit test 2 to check the matching section of the advanced short answer unit test. There is no key for the short answer questions. The answers will be based on the discussions you have had during class.

There are two multiple choice unit tests. Following the two unit tests, you will find an answer sheet on which students should mark their answers. The same answer sheet should be used for both tests; however, students' answers will be different for each test. Following the students' answer sheet for the multiple choice tests you will find your answer keys.

The short answer tests have a vocabulary section. You should choose 10 of the vocabulary words from this unit, read them orally and have the students write them down. Then, either have students write a definition or use the words in sentences. The second part of the vocabulary test is matching.

LESSON TWENTY

Student Objectives
1. To widen the breadth of students' knowledge about the topics discussed or touched upon in *The River*
2. To check students' non-fiction assignments

Activity

Ask each student to give a brief oral report about the nonfiction work he/she read for the nonfiction assignment. Your criteria for evaluating this report will vary depending on the level of your students. You may wish for students to give a complete report without using notes of any kind, or you may want students to read directly from a written report, or you may want to do something in between these two extremes. Just make students aware of your criteria in ample time for them to prepare their reports.

Start with one student's report, After that, ask if anyone else in the class has read on a topic related to the first student's report. If no one has, choose another student at random. After each report, be sure to ask if anyone has a report related to the one just completed. That will help keep a continuity during the discussion of the reports.

UNIT TESTS

SHORT ANSWER UNIT TEST 1 *The River*

1. Matching/ Identify

____ 1. tension   A. Brian's only tool
____ 2. belt knife   B. Brian's main problem in wilderness
____ 3. food   C. was not accurate
____ 4. lightning   D. didn't go on the second trip
____ 5. map   E. knocked out the radio
____ 6. raft   F. transportation to the trading post
____ 7. government   G. gift from Derek to Brian
____ 8. canoe   H. the trip was lacking it
____ 9. hunger   I. wanted improved survival training
____ 10. hatchet   J. most important, according to Brian

II. Short Answer

1. What were some of the changes in Brian since his first time in the wilderness?

2. What did Brian tell Derek about teaching people to survive in the wilderness?

Short Answer Unit Test 1 *The River*

3. Describe the first day and night of the trip down the river.

4. What did Brian do, in order, when he found the raft and Derek after they had gone through the water chute?

5. Describe the significance of the following quotation: ""Next time, it won't be so hard to paddle. Thanks."

Short Answer Unit Test 1 *The River*

III. Fill-In-the-Blank Write the word or words to correctly complete each sentence about the story.

1. Brian Robeson had already survived alone in the wilderness for fifty-four days. Now the _____ wanted him to do it again.

2. This time, Derek Holtzer, a _____, was going along to record Brian's thoughts and actions.

3. Brian insisted that they make the trip as real as possible, so the only gear the took was their _____, a _____, and Derek's _____ and notebooks.

4. On their third night, a storm came up. Lightning hit Derek and put him in a _____.

5. Brian read the map in the briefcase and saw that there was a _____ down the river.

6. He made a _____, tied Derek on, and set out for help.

7. They went through a chute that was like a waterfall. Brian _____.

8. Brian and Derek were finally rescued by _____.

9. Brian lost 12 pounds and had an infection in his _____, but it cleared up.

10. Derek _____ in about six months.

Short Answer Unit Test 1 *The River*

IV. <u>Essay</u> Draw and label a plot diagram of the story. Include all important events from the story.

Short Answer Unit Test 1 *The River*

V. <u>Vocabulary Part 1</u>

Listen to the vocabulary words and spell them. After you have spelled all the words, go back and write down the definitions.

WORD	**DEFINITION**
1.	
2.	
3.	
4.	
5.	
6.	
7.	
8.	
9.	
10.	

<u>Vocabulary Part 2</u> Directions: Place the letter of the matching definition on the blank line.

____	1.	crude	A.	ruled out
____	2.	aspect	B.	an indentation or small hollow
____	3.	externalize	C.	glassy-eyed
____	4.	exasperation	D.	a way of looking at something
____	5.	negated	E.	to show outwardly
____	6.	indication	F.	promised
____	7.	glazed	G.	roughly made
____	8.	careening	H.	annoyance
____	9.	alcove	I.	rushing headlong
____	10.	vowed	J.	a sign or suggestion

ANSWER KEY SHORT ANSWER UNIT TEST 1 *The River*

1. <u>Matching/ Identify</u>

H	1.	tension	A.	Brian's only tool
A	2.	belt knife	B.	Brian's main problem in wilderness
J	3.	food	C.	was not accurate
E	4.	lightning	D.	didn't go on the second trip
C	5.	map	E.	knocked out the radio
F	6.	raft	F.	transportation to the trading post
I	7.	government	G.	gift from Derek to Brian
G	8.	canoe	H.	the trip was lacking it
B	9.	hunger	I.	wanted improved survival training
D	10.	hatchet	J.	most important, according to Brian

II. <u>Short Answer</u>

1. What were some of the changes in Brian since his first time in the wilderness?
   He liked to cook. He became closer to his mother, and admired her. He learned to accept things. He became evasive when talking about his time in the wilderness.

2. What did Brian tell Derek about teaching people to survive in the wilderness?
   He said it wouldn't work unless each person actually had to try and survive. Just telling them wouldn't work.

3. Describe the beginning of the trip down the river, from the time Brian left until the first night.
   It was difficult. The raft was hard to turn, and Brian often ran into the bank. He learned to paddle through the curves and kept the raft mostly on course. He found that his time estimate was short, and re-estimated that the trip would take 50 hours.
   During the night, Brian was tired. He would fall asleep between paddle strokes. At one point he fell asleep and woke up to find the raft in a lake. He began paddling out of the lake. He stayed awake, but began to hallucinate.

4. What did Brian do, in order, when he found the raft?
   He made sure Derek was breathing. Then he either fell asleep or was unconscious across Derek. When he woke up he made a new paddle. He paddled all day and all night.

5. Describe the significance of the following quotation: "Next time, it won't be so hard to paddle. Thanks."

About seven months after the trip, Brian received a Kevlar canoe and paddles. The note was inside the canoe, and was signed "Derek."

III. <u>Fill-In-the-Blank</u>

1. Brian Robeson had already survived alone in the wilderness for fifty-four days. Now the **government** wanted him to do it again.

2. This time, Derek Holtzer, a **psychologist**, was going along to record Brian's thoughts and actions.

3. Brian insisted that they make the trip as real as possible, so the only gear they took was their **pocket knives,** a **radio**, and Derek's **briefcase** and notebooks.

4. On their third night, a storm came up. Lightning hit Derek and put him in a **coma**.

5. Brian read the map in the briefcase and saw that there was a **trading post** down the river.

6. He made a **raft** tied Derek on, and set out for help.

7. They went through a chute that was like a waterfall. Brian **was thrown off**.

8. Brian and Derek were finally rescued by **a man and woman from the trading post**.

9. Brian lost 12 pounds and had an infection in his **hands,** but it cleared up.

10. Derek **recovered completely** in about six months.

IV. <u>Essay</u> The answers will depend on class discussions.

V. <u>Vocabulary</u> Choose ten words to read orally for Part One of the test.

G	1.	crude	A.	ruled out
D	2.	aspect	B.	an indentation or small hollow
E	3.	externalize	C.	glassy-eyed
H	4.	exasperation	D.	a way of looking at something
A	5.	negated	E.	to show outwardly
J	6.	indication	F.	promised
C	7.	glazed	G.	roughly made
I	8.	careening	H.	annoyance
B	9.	alcove	I.	rushing headlong
F	10.	vowed	J.	a sign or suggestion

SHORT ANSWER UNIT TEST 2 *The River*

I. Matching/Identify

___ 1. map   A. Brian's only tool
___ 2. raft   B. gift from Derek to Brian
___ 3. government   C. transportation to the trading post
___ 4. belt knife   D. Brian's main problem in wilderness
___ 5. lightning   E. the trip was lacking it
___ 6. tension   F. wanted improved survival training
___ 7. hunger   G. most important, according to Brian
___ 8. hatchet   H. knocked out the radio
___ 9. canoe   I. didn't go on the second trip
___ 10. food   J. was not accurate

II. Short Answer

1. How did Brian's mother react to Derek's request?

2. What did Brian tell Derek about the gear? How did they solve the problem? What did Derek say about it later on?

Short Answer Unit Test 2 *The River*

3. What was the "bad thinking?" What did Brian do about it?.

4. How were Brian and Derek rescued? What was Brian's reaction to the rescue?

5. Describe the significance of the following quotation: "I don't know--it's just wrong, I think. "

Short Answer Unit Test 2 *The River*

III. <u>Fill-In-the-Blank</u>   Write the word or words to correctly complete each sentence about the story.

1. About a year after Brian Robeson was rescued from the wilderness, the government asked him to go into the wilderness again so he could _____ them what it was like.
2. Derek Holtzer, a psychologist, went along so he could _____ Brian's thoughts and actions.
3. When he stepped out of the plane onto the dry grass, Brian _____.
4. On the third night, there was a storm and Derek was _____.
5. At first, Brian thought he could wait for help. Then, when Derek was not able to _____, Brian was afraid he would die of dehydration.
6. Brian made a raft, put Derek on it, and set out for the _____ down the river.
7. On the third morning Brian discovered that the map was _____.
8. The raft went through a _____ and Brian was thrown off.
9. Brian _____ until he found Derek and the raft again.
10. They were rescued by _____, and both recovered from the experience.

IV. <u>Essay</u>   Explain the statement: He became something other than himself that afternoon.

Short Answer Unit Test 2 *The River*

V. <u>Vocabulary Part 1</u>

Listen to the vocabulary words and spell them. After you have spelled all the words, go back and write down the definitions.

WORD	**DEFINITION**
1.	
2.	
3.	
4.	
5.	
6.	
7.	
8.	
9.	
10.	

<u>Vocabulary Part 2</u>   Match the word and the definition.

_____ 1. precaution   A. muffled; softened
_____ 2. vetoed   B. to return to a former condition
_____ 3. revert   C. shocked
_____ 4. horde   D. rejected; refused
_____ 5. prying   E. eased off
_____ 6. lurched   F. rolled; dipped down
_____ 7. stunned   G. a large group; a swarm
_____ 8. buffeted   H. safeguard
_____ 9. muted   I. hit; beat
_____ 10. relented   J. looking curiously; snooping

ANSWER KEY SHORT ANSWER UNIT TEST 2 *The River*

I. Matching/Identify

Note: Also use this key for the Advanced Short Answer Unit Test.

J	1.	map	A.	Brian's only tool
C	2.	raft	B.	gift from Derek to Brian
F	3.	government	C.	transportation to the trading post
A	4.	belt knife	D.	Brian's main problem in wilderness
H	5.	lightning	E.	the trip was lacking it
E	6.	tension	F.	wanted improved survival training
D	7.	hunger	G.	most important, according to Brian
I	8.	hatchet	H.	knocked out the radio
B	9.	canoe	I.	didn't go on the second trip
G	10.	food	J.	was not accurate

II. Short Answer

1. How did Brian's mother react to the request?
   At first she said it was insane. She agreed after she realized Brian really wanted to do it, and Derek assured her it would be safe.

2. What did Brian tell Derek about the gear? How did they solve the problem? What did Derek say about it later on?
   Brian said if they unloaded the gear, he would go home. They compromised and took their belt knives, a radio, and Derek's briefcase and notebooks. Later on, Derek admitted that Brian was right.

3. What was the "bad thinking?" What did Brian do about it?
   After two nights without sleep, Brian began thinking that it would be better if Derek were gone. He screamed "No", touched Derek's leg and mumbled that they would go all of the way together.

4. How were they rescued? What was Brian's reaction to the rescue?
   Brian paddled until he reached the trading post. A dog there alerted a young boy who ran to the trading post for help. A man and woman pulled him out of the water. He was crying as they helped him. The man jumped in and took care of Derek.

5. Describe the significance of the following quotation: "I don't know--it's just wrong, I think."
   On the third day of their trip, Brian told Derek things were too easy. They were all ready and calm. It didn't seem real to him.

III. Fill-In-the-Blank

1. About a year after Brian Robeson was rescued from the wilderness, the government asked him to go into the wilderness again so he could **teach** them what it was like.
2. Derek Holtzer, a psychologist, went along so he could **record** Brian's thoughts and actions.
3. When he stepped out of the plane onto the dry grass, Brian **changed completely**.
4. On the third night, there was a storm and Derek was **struck by lightning/put into a coma after being hit by lightning.**.
5. At first, Brian thought he could wait for help. Then, when Derek was not able to **swallow water**, Brian was afraid he would die of dehydration.
6. Brian made a raft, put Derek on it, and set out for the **trading post** down the river.
7. On the third morning Brian discovered that the map was **inaccurate**.
8. The raft went through a **chute/waterfall** and Brian was thrown off.
9. Brian **swam** until he found Derek and the raft again.
10. They were rescued by **a man and woman at the trading post** and both recovered from the experience.

IV. Essay   The answers will depend on class discussions.

V. Vocabulary Read ten words orally for Part One.

H	1.	precaution	A.	muffled; softened
D	2.	vetoed	B.	to return to a former condition
B	3.	revert	C.	shocked
G	4.	horde	D.	rejected; refused
J	5.	prying	E.	eased off
F	6.	lurched	F.	rolled; dipped down
C	7.	stunned	G.	a large group; a swarm
I	8.	buffeted	H.	safeguard
A	9.	muted	I.	hit; beat
E	10.	relented	J.	looking curiously; snooping

ADVANCED SHORT ANSWER UNIT TEST *THE RIVER*

I. Matching/Identify

____ 1. map   A. Brian's only tool
____ 2. raft   B. gift from Derek to Brian
____ 3. government   C. transportation to the trading post
____ 4. belt knife   D. Brian's main problem in wilderness
____ 5. lightning   E. the trip was lacking it
____ 6. tension   F. wanted improved survival training
____ 7. hunger   G. most important, according to Brian
____ 8. hatchet   H. knocked out the radio
____ 9. canoe   I. didn't go on the second trip
____ 10. food   J. was not accurate

II. Short Answer

1. What are the main conflicts in the story? Are they resolved? If so, how? If not, why not?

2. Why did Brian think the easy time was all wrong? What does this tell about his character?

Advanced Short Answer Unit Test *The River*

3. What was the greatest danger that Brian faced? Why do you think so?

4. Identify a few examples of simile and discuss their contribution to the novel.

5. Brian has already shown that he can survive in the wilderness. How does Gary Paulsen hold the reader's interest as Brian goes into the wilderness for the second time? Use examples from the story to support your answer.

Advanced Short Answer Unit Test *The River*

III. <u>Quotations</u>   Directions: Discuss the significance of the following quotations

1. "But that's crazy. It was . . . rough. I mean, I almost died and it was just luck that I made it out."

2. "I was just . . . looking at things. Seeing them."

3. *I can't do this*, he thought. *I can't do this alone. I just can't.*

Advanced Short Answer Unit Test *The River*

4. "We go."

5. "Next time," he read aloud, "it won't be so hard to paddle. Thanks."

Advanced Short Answer Unit Test *The River*

IV. Vocabulary

Listen to the words and write them down. After you have written down all of the words, write a paragraph in which you use all of the words. The paragraph must in some way relate to *The River*.

1. _____ 6. _____
2. _____ 7. _____
3. _____ 8. _____
4. _____ 9. _____
5. _____ 10. _____

MULTIPLE CHOICE UNIT TEST 1 *The River*

I. Matching/Identify

___ 1. tension   A. Brian's only tool
___ 2. belt knife   B. Brian's main problem in wilderness
___ 3. food   C. was not accurate
___ 4. lightning   D. didn't go on the second trip
___ 5. map   E. knocked out the radio
___ 6. raft   F. transportation to the trading post
___ 7. government   G. gift from Derek to Brian
___ 8. canoe   H. the trip was lacking it
___ 9. hunger   I. wanted improved survival training
___ 10. hatchet   J. most important, according to Brian

II. Multiple Choice

1. How long after The Time does this story take place?
   A. It takes place two years after he was rescued.
   B. It takes place one year after he was rescued.
   C. It takes place six months after he was rescued.
   D. It takes place a year and a half after he was rescued.

2. True or False: Derek asked Brian to think out loud so he could record the thoughts in his notebook.
   A. True
   B. False

3. What, according to Brian, was everything?
   A. Bravery was everything.
   B. Sleep was everything.
   C. Food was everything.
   D. Shelter was everything.

4. True or False: Brian thought the trip was going very well after the first three days.
   A. True
   B. False

Multiple Choice Unit Test 1 *The River*

5. What was the distance from the lake to the trading post? How long did Brian think it would take to get there?
    A. The trading post was about 100 miles or 150 kilometers from the lake. Brian estimated it would take 35 to 40 hours to make the trip.
    B. The trading post was about 200 miles or 320 kilometers from the lake. Brian estimated it would take 50 to 60 hours to make the trip.
    C. The trading post was about 50 miles or 81 kilometers from the lake. Brian estimated it would take 20 to 25 hours to make the trip.
    D. The trading post was about 150 miles or 243 kilometers from the lake. Brian estimated it would take 45 to 50 hours to make the trip.

6. What was Brian's main problem?
    A. He thought Derek needed constant watching. He couldn't figure out how to watch Derek and build the raft at the same time.
    B. He had never built a raft, and didn't know how to do it.
    C. The logs he found were too heavy for him to lift by himself. He needed help, and he didn't have it.
    D. He didn't have a tool to use to make the raft. All he had were the two knives, and he couldn't use them to cut through the logs.

7. What did Brian do just before he started down the river?
    A. He started a slow burning signal fire near their campsite.
    B. He gathered enough food for a week and put it on the raft.
    C. He made a signal marker out of stones and branches to show which way they had gone.
    D. He left a note in the plastic case with the radio and tied it under the overhang.

8. What happened because of Brian's physical condition during the first night?
    A. He fell asleep and fell off the raft.
    B. He was in good shape and paddled almost fifteen miles.
    C. He tried to stay awake and began to hallucinate.
    D. His arms got so sore he could not paddle. He had to let the raft drift.

9. What did Brian do **first** when he found the raft?
    A. He either fell asleep or fell unconscious across Derek.
    B. He fixed the raft.
    C. He began paddling immediately.
    D. He made sure Derek was breathing.

Multiple Choice Unit Test 1 *The River*

10. Which of the following is true?
    A. Brian did not have any long range difficulties from the trip.
    B. Brian lost 25 pounds on the trip.
    C. Brian's feet were infected from bacteria in the lake but they toughened up.
    D. Brian's mother sued the government for not protecting her son from danger.

III. Vocabulary Part 1

___ 1.	crude	A.	ruled out
___ 2.	aspect	B.	an indentation or small hollow
___ 3.	externalize	C.	glassy-eyed
___ 4.	exasperation	D.	a way of looking at something
___ 5.	negated	E.	to show outwardly
___ 6.	indication	F.	promised
___ 7.	glazed	G.	roughly made
___ 8.	careening	H.	annoyance
___ 9.	alcove	I.	rushing headlong
___ 10.	vowed	J.	a sign or suggestion

Multiple Choice Unit Test 1 *The River*

Vocabulary Part 2   Directions: Write the letter of the word that matches the definition.

1. **misleading**
   a. skimpy
   b. evasive
   c. submerged
   d. perversely

2. **safeguard**
   a. alcove
   b. chute
   c. cue
   d. precaution

3. **enormous**
   a. doubts
   b. massive
   c. accurate
   d. flexed

4. **to return to a former condition**
   a. compromise
   b. horde
   c. revert
   d. fend

5. **fall apart**
   a. lurched
   b. vetoed
   c. disintegrate
   d. prying

6. **to silence**
   a. thrive
   b. squelch
   c. revert
   d. chute

7. **shocked**
   a. marooned
   b. negated
   c. stunned
   d. lurched

8. **exact**
   a. accurate
   b. compromise
   c. buffeted
   d. enhanced

9. **fight against**
   a. clambered
   b. fend
   c. externalize
   d. evasive

10. **heavy block of iron or steel**
    a. cue
    b. alcove
    c. coma
    d. anvil

Multiple Choice Unit Test 1 *The River*

IV. <u>Quotations</u>   Directions: Write the letter of the word or phrase that completes the quotation.

_____	1.	"Out here, . . . ___ is everything."	A.	ethics
_____	2.	"We're so ready, so calm. It ___."	B.	mosquitoes
_____	3.	"You can't have too much ___."	C.	food
_____	4.	"We want you to ___."	D.	do this alone
_____	5.	"I admire his ___."	E.	wood
_____	6.	"Next time, it won't be so hard to ___."	F.	together
_____	7.	"We go all the way ___."	G.	doesn't work
_____	8.	"___. It's so. . . so alive."	H.	fire
_____	9.	"No more ___."	I.	do it again
_____	10.	"I can't ___."	J.	paddle

MULTIPLE CHOICE UNIT TEST 2 *The River*

I. <u>Matching/Identify</u>

____ 1.	map	A.	Brian's only tool
____ 2.	raft	B.	gift from Derek to Brian
____ 3.	government	C.	transportation to the trading post
____ 4.	belt knife	D.	Brian's main problem in wilderness
____ 5.	lightning	E.	the trip was lacking it
____ 6.	tension	F.	wanted improved survival training
____ 7.	hunger	G.	most important, according to Brian
____ 8.	hatchet	H.	knocked out the radio
____ 9.	canoe	I.	didn't go on the second trip
____ 10.	food	J.	was not accurate

II. <u>Multiple Choice</u>

1. Who was Derek Holtzer and what did he want?
    A. He was a tour promoter from a resort club. He wanted to develop some wilderness tours, and asked Brian to serve as the consultant and spokesperson for the group.
    B. He was an author who wanted to write a book about Brian's adventures in the wilderness.
    C. He was a psychologist from a government survival school. He wanted Brian to go into the wilderness again, so they could learn from him and teach their students.
    D. He was a clothing manufacturer who wanted to make clothes with Brian's name on them.

2. Which was **not** one of the changes in Brian since his time in the wilderness?
    A. He became closer to his mother, and admired her.
    B. He liked to cook.
    C. He became evasive when talking about his time in the wilderness.
    D. He became nervous and jittery in small, closed-in places.

3. What happened to Brian as he stepped out of the plane onto dry grass?
    A. He changed completely. He became what he had been before at the lake.
    B. He took a deep breath and told Derek he had missed the wilderness.
    C. He had a panic attack and ran back into the plane.
    D. He started crying and said he didn't know if he could go through with it.

Multiple Choice Unit Test 2 *The River*

4. What did Derek say about the trip?
    A. He said it was not as hard as he thought it would be.
    B. He said the trip lacked tension.
    C. He said it was going just as he expected, and he was very pleased.
    D. He said it was boring, and not at all what he expected.

5. What did Brian find in the briefcase? What did he decide to do?
    A. He found a notebook and wrote down everything that had happened since the storm.
    B. He found a second radio that Derek had hidden. He decided to call for help.
    C. He found a map that showed the lake, the river that flowed out of it, and a trading post. He decided to make a raft and take Derek to the trading post.
    D. He found a schedule that showed someone would be calling them in three more days. He decided to continue waiting for help.

6. What was Brian's main problem while building the raft?
    A. He thought Derek needed constant watching. He couldn't figure out how to watch Derek and build the raft at the same time.
    B. He had never built a raft, and didn't know how to do it.
    C. The logs he found were too heavy for him to lift by himself. He needed help, and he didn't have it.
    D. He didn't have a tool to use to make the raft. All he had were the two knives, and he couldn't use them to cut through the logs.

7. What did Brian do just before he started down the river?
    A. He left a note in the plastic case with the radio and tied it under the overhang.
    B. He gathered enough food for a week and put it on the raft.
    C. He made a signal marker out of stones and branches to show which way they had gone.
    D. He started a slow burning signal fire near their campsite.

8. True or False: The first part of the trip was easy. The raft stayed on course and was easy to steer.
    A. True
    B. False

Multiple Choice Unit Test 2 *The River*

9. What was the "bad thinking?" that Brian experienced two nights without sleep? What did Brian do about it?
   A. Brian thought it would be better to leave Derek in a sheltered spot near the river bank. He made a small lean-to, and left Derek there while he went for help.
   B. Brian thought he had made a mistake and would never find the trading post. He thought about turning back, but decided to go on.
   C. Brian began thinking that it would be better if Derek were gone. He screamed "No", touched Derek's leg and mumbled that they would go all of the way together.
   D. Brian was too tired to go on. He thought about resting where he was for a day or two. Then he realized he had to get to the trading post..

10. Which of the following did **not** happen?
    A. The raft went through a chute that was like a waterfall.
    B. The jacket strips that tied Derek came loose and he fell off.
    C. The raft struck a submerged boulder.
    D. Brian was caught in the pressure wave from the chute.

Vocabulary Part 1   Match the word and the definition.

_____ 1. precaution   A. muffled; softened
_____ 2. vetoed   B. to return to a former condition
_____ 3. revert   C. shocked
_____ 4. horde   D. rejected; refused
_____ 5. prying   E. eased off
_____ 6. lurched   F. rolled; dipped down
_____ 7. stunned   G. a large group; a swarm
_____ 8. buffeted   H. safeguard
_____ 9. muted   I. hit; beat
_____ 10. relented   J. looking curiously; snooping

Multiple Choice Unit Test 2 *The River*

Vocabulary Part 2   Directions: Write the letter of the word that matches the definition.

1. **to set right; correct**
   a. disintegrate
   b. thrive
   c. submerged
   d. rectify

2. **sturdy**
   a. stable
   b. perversely
   c. glazed
   d. skimpy

3. **way of looking at something**
   a. aspect
   b. rectify
   c. indication
   d. muted

4. **improved**
   a. negated
   b. stunned
   c. enhanced
   d. clambered

5. **annoyance**
   a. exasperation
   b. cue
   c. compromise
   d. indication

6. **loss of water or moisture**
   a. compromise
   b. **dehydration**
   c. glazed
   d. coma

7. **misleading**
   a. marooned
   b. stable
   c. accurate
   d. evasive

8. **rolled; dipped down**
   a. vowed
   b. submerged
   c. lurched
   d. pulverized

9. **hit; beat**
   a. careening
   b. buffeted
   c. embedded
   d. disintegrate

10. **curious looking; snooping**
    a. rectify
    b. careening
    c. prying
    d. indication

Multiple Choice Unit Test 2 *The River*

IV. Quotations   Directions: Write the letter of the word or phrase that completes the quotation.

_____ 1.	"You had something more . . . besides ___."	A. swim
_____ 2.	"I truly and honestly discovered ___."	B. thunder
_____ 3.	"That's what nature is, really-- getting ___."	C. together
_____ 4.	No sound could be loud enough to get over the __.	D. food
_____ 5.	*Let's ___ it out*, he thought, his mind blurred as his vision.	E. knife
_____ 6.	"It's just under a hundred miles to the ___."	F. reason
_____ 7.	"I'll have to ___."	G. fire
_____ 8.	"Next time, it won't be so hard to ___."	H. paddle
_____ 9.	"We go all the way ___."	I. trading post
_____ 10.	"Lots of people carry a ___ of some kind."	J. luck

ANSWER SHEET Multiple Choice Unit Tests *The River*

I. Matching

1. _____
2. _____
3. _____
4. _____
5. _____
6. _____
7. _____
8. _____
9. _____
10. _____

II. Multiple Choice

1. (A) (B) (C) (D)
2. (A) (B) (C) (D)
3. (A) (B) (C) (D)
4. (A) (B) (C) (D)
5. (A) (B) (C) (D)
6. (A) (B) (C) (D)
7. (A) (B) (C) (D)
8. (A) (B) (C) (D)
9. (A) (B) (C) (D)
10. (A) (B) (C) (D)

III. Quotations

1. _____
2. _____
3. _____
4. _____
5. _____
6. _____
7. _____
8. _____
9. _____
10. _____

IV. Vocabulary Part 1

1. _____
2. _____
3. _____
4. _____
5. _____
6. _____
7. _____
8. _____
9. _____
10. _____

Vocabulary Part 2

1. _____
2. _____
3. _____
4. _____
5. _____
6. _____
7. _____
8. _____
9. _____
10. _____

ANSWER SHEET KEY Multiple Choice Unit Test 1 *The River*

I. Matching

1. H
2. A
3. J
4. E
5. C
6. F
7. I
8. G
9. B
10. D

II. Multiple Choice

1. (A) ( ) (C) (D)
2. ( ) (B) (C) (D)
3. (A) (B) ( ) (D)
4. (A) ( ) (C) (D)
5. ( ) (B) (C) (D)
6. (A) (B) (C) ( )
7. (A) (B) (C) ( )
8. (A) (B) ( ) (D)
9. (A) (B) (C) ( )
10. ( ) (B) (C) (D)

III. Quotations

1. C
2. G
3. E
4. I
5. A
6. J
7. F
8. H
9. B
10. D

IV. Vocabulary Part 1

1. G
2. D
3. E
4. H
5. A
6. J
7. C
8. I
9. B
10. F

Vocabulary Part 2

1. B
2. D
3. A
4. C
5. C
6. B
7. C
8. A
9. B
10. D

ANSWER SHEET KEY   Multiple Choice Unit Test 2 *The River*

I. Matching

1. J
2. C
3. F
4. A
5. H
6. E
7. D
8. I
9. B
10. G

II. Multiple Choice

1. (A) (B) ( ) (D)
2. (A) (B) (C) ( )
3. ( ) (B) (C) (D)
4. (A) ( ) (C) (D)
5. (A) (B) ( ) (D)
6. (A) (B) (C) ( )
7. ( ) (B) (C) (D)
8. (A) ( ) (C) (D)
9. (A) (B) ( ) (D)
10. (A) ( ) (C) (D)

III. Quotations

1. J
2. G
3. D
4. B
5. F
6. I
7. A
8. H
9. C
10. E

IV. Vocabulary Part 1

1. H
2. D
3. B
4. G
5. J
6. F
7. C
8. I
9. A
10. E

Vocabulary Part 2

1. D
2. A
3. A
4. C
5. A
6. B
7. D
8. C
9. B
10. C

UNIT RESOURCES

BULLETIN BOARD IDEAS *The River*

1. Save one corner of the board for the best of students' *The River* writing assignments. You may want to use background maps of New York and Canada to represent the setting of the novel.

2. Take one of the word search puzzles from the extra activities packet and with a marker copy it over in a large size on the bulletin board. Write the clue words to find to one side. Invite students prior to and after class to find the words and circle them on the bulletin board.

3. Have students find or draw pictures that they think resemble the people and scenery in the book.

4. Invite students to help make an interactive bulletin board quiz. Give each student a half-sheet of paper (about 4"x5') folded in half so that it can open. On the outside flap, have each student write a description of one of the characters in the text. On the inside, they will write the name of the character. You can staple or tack these papers to the bulletin board so that the students can read the descriptions and lift the flaps to find the answers.

5. Collect and display pictures of the Canadian wilderness.

6. Display contour maps of various areas.

7. Display pictures and descriptions of small airplanes and hand tools.

8. Display articles about Gary Paulsen.

9. Have students design postcards depicting the settings of the book.

10. Display a contour map of northeastern Canada and have students mark the route that Brian's raft may have taken.

EXTRA ACTIVITIES *The River*

One of the difficulties in teaching a novel is that all students don't read at the same speed. One student who likes to read may take the book home and finish it in a day or two. Sometimes a few students finish the in-class assignments early. The problem, then, is finding suitable extra activities for students.

One thing that helps is to keep a library in the classroom. For this unit on *The River* you might check out from the school or public library other books by Gary Paulsen. There are also many other survival and coming-of-age novels that students would enjoy reading. Magazines such as *Boy's Life* and *National Geographic World* contain articles about wilderness areas and young adults who do interesting things. Several journals have critiques of Paulsen's works. Some of the students may enjoy reading these and responding either in writing or in discussion groups.

Your students who have reading difficulties, or speak English as a second language, may benefit from listening to all or part of the book on tape. *The River* is available commercially, or you may want to have an adult or a student who reads well tape record the book for you.

Other things you may keep on hand are word search puzzles. Several puzzles relating directly to *The River* are included in the unit. Feel free to duplicate them.

Some students may like to draw. You might devise a contest or allow some extra-credit grade for students who draw characters or scenes from *The River*. Note, too, that if the students do not want to keep their drawings you may pick up some extra bulletin board materials this way. If you have a contest and you supply the prize. You could, possibly, make the drawing itself a non-refundable entry fee.

Have maps, a globe, and travel brochures on hand for easy reference. Travel agencies and automobile clubs are good sources for these materials.

The pages which follow contain games, puzzles, and worksheets. The keys, when appropriate, immediately follow the puzzle or worksheet. There are two main groups of activities: one group for the unit; that is, generally relating to the *The River* text, and another group of activities related strictly to the *The River* vocabulary.

Directions for the games, puzzles, and worksheets are self-explanatory. The object here is to provide you with extra materials you may use in any way you choose.

MORE ACTIVITIES *The River*

1. Pick one of the incidents for students to dramatize. Encourage students to write dialog for the characters. (Perhaps you could assign various episodes to different groups of students so more than one episode could be acted and more students could participate.)

2. Have students design a bulletin board for *The River*

3. Invite a Scout troop leader or an older Scout to talk to the class about wilderness survival.

4. If you live near a military base, you may be able to have someone from the base come and talk about their survival training.

5. Ask someone from the Red Cross or the local paramedics to talk to the class about survival techniques, especially what to do if someone is in a coma.

6. Have students work in pairs to create an interview with one of the characters. One student should be the interviewer and the other should be the interviewee. Students can work together to compose questions for the interviewer to ask. Each pair of students could present their interview to the class in the form of a talk show

7. Invite students who have read other books by Gary Paulsen to present booktalks to the class.

8. Invite students who have read a biography of Gary Paulsen to tell the class about his life.

9. Use some of the related topics (noted earlier for an in-class library) as topics for research, reports, or written papers, or as topics for guest speakers.

10. Invite a story teller to tell one or more stories related to *The River* to the class.

11. Have students hold small group discussions related to topics in the book. Assign a recorder and a speaker for each group. Have the speaker from each group make a report to the class.

12. Have students work in small groups to write a sequel telling what happened to Brian after he returned from his trip with Derek.

13. Have students write a report on the trip from Derek's point of view.

14. Have students write a survival plan of their own. This could be based on any natural or man-made disaster.

15. Have students draw a contour map of their city or state.

16. Paulsen mentioned the distances down the river in miles and kilometers. Have the students calculate various distances in miles and kilometers.

17. Have students work with an adult (outside of class time) to build a raft similar to the one Brian made.

18. Invite someone with two-way radios to give a demonstration to the class.

The River Word Search

```
R O B E S O N K X V S C I H T E R R G
O X T J Y S S B A B R O G Q X W E A N
B S W H L E N P Q T R M R N K G O S L
E H E M G O E X T L I A S A N Z T P R
S F L I N T E K C A J E N U D L C B Z
O N V V I I T S R G V E H N A I L E T
N G E S N U F R T I V V C V O T O R X
Z C Y V T Q I P N E R M I D R C D R G
B O U G H S F K S E S V E N H G K I Q
M U M X G O P G Z M R M E I T K C E N
S N F X I M G T S U I W S B R T G S L
T S M X L R L R S T X M A N N E R L Y
R E W T C O N Q U N G L C R B Z P R M
D L N R H E B D C B L Y F Y I W Y A W
N O C S S B N A N A W X E G R T Q L B
B R H L I K N L R P B O I E C T W P H
S F U C O O K D D E B O R A H F O O D
N A T R E D N C X Q G I B M K A O P Q
P B E A V E R S I X F M A P S R D F D
```

BALLARD	COOK	HOLTZER	NECKTIE	SIX
BEAVERS	COUNSELOR	HUNGER	PAULSEN	SURVIVAL
BIRCH	DEBORAH	JACKET	POPLAR	TENSION
BOUGHS	ETHICS	KATIE	RADIO	TIME
BRANNOCK	FIFTEEN	KNIVES	RAFT	TWELVE
BRIEFCASE	FIRE	LIGHTNING	RASPBERRIES	TWO
CANOE	FLINT	MANNERLY	ROBESON	TWO
CHUTE	FOOD	MAP	ROBESON	WOOD
COMA	GRUBWORMS	MOSQUITOES	SEVEN	

The River Word Search Answer Key

```
R O B E S O N K       S C I H T E       R
O   T     S     A B   O         W E     A
B   W     S E   N T R M R       G O     S
E   E     G O E   I A S A N       D     P
S F L I N T E K C A J E N U D L         B
O   V     I I T     V E H N A I         E
N   E     N U F     I   V   V O         R
    C     T Q I   N E R     I     C     R
B O U G H S   F K S E   V E     K       I
    U       G   O     Z R M E I T K C E N
    N       I   M G T U I   S B         S
T   S       L   L R S T M A N N E R L Y
    E           O N   U   L C   B       R
    L       H E     C B   F   I         A
    O   C   S S   A   A W E   R T       L
    R H L I   N   R   O I E C T W       P
    U   C O O K D D E B O R A H F O O   D
    A   T   E   N         I B   M   A O P
P   B E A V E R S   I X F M A P S   R D
```

BALLARD	COOK	HOLTZER	NECKTIE	SIX
BEAVERS	COUNSELOR	HUNGER	PAULSEN	SURVIVAL
BIRCH	DEBORAH	JACKET	POPLAR	TENSION
BOUGHS	ETHICS	KATIE	RADIO	TIME
BRANNOCK	FIFTEEN	KNIVES	RAFT	TWELVE
BRIEFCASE	FIRE	LIGHTNING	RASPBERRIES	TWO
CANOE	FLINT	MANNERLY	ROBESON	TWO
CHUTE	FOOD	MAP	ROBESON	WOOD
COMA	GRUBWORMS	MOSQUITOES	SEVEN	

The River Crossword

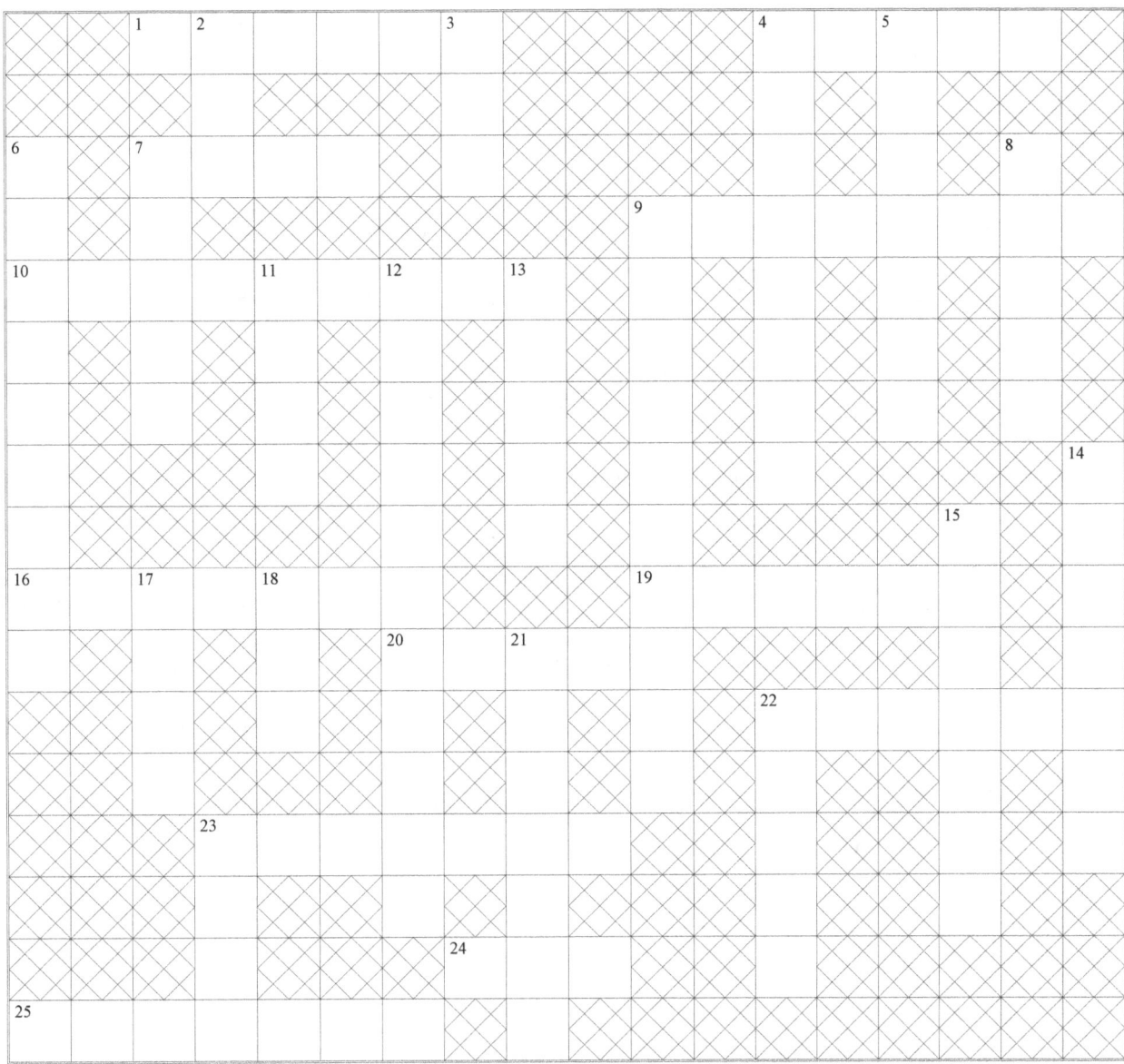

Across
1. Derek admired Brian's
4. ____bark; used for food containers
7. Derek's medical state
9. Bill____ said the government wanted Brian to teach them
10. Possible food
16. Name of the river
19. Pounds Brian lost
20. Left behind on trip down the river
22. Their only tools
23. Brian ____; two-time wilderness survivor
24. Showed the way to the trading post
25. Derek ____; psychologist who went with Brian

Down
2. Speed in mph the raft traveled
3. Months for Derek to recover
4. Name of trading post
5. Mr. ____; was about to get married
6. Caused the problems on the trip
7. Dangerous, rocky water
8. Needed to make a fire
9. Attacked the first night
11. Brian said there could never be too much of it
12. First Food
13. Months after trip when Brian received Derek's gift
14. Author
15. Cut the trees that Brian used for the raft
17. Brian's new hobby after first time in the wilderness
18. Katie ____; Brian and Derek's code name
21. ____McKenzie; Brian's girlfriend
22. ____ONE; radio station code name
23. Name of the canoe

The River Crossword Answer Key

		1 E	2 T	H	I	C	S			4 B	5 I	R	C	H	
			W				I			R		O			
6 L	7 C	O	M	A		X				A		B		8 F	
I	H							9 M	A	N	N	E	R	L	Y
10 G	R	U	11 B	12 W	O	R	13 M	O		N		S		I	
H	T		O	A			E	S		O		O		N	
T	E		O	S			V	Q		C		N		T	
N			D	P			E	U		K				14 P	
I				B			N	I				15 B		A	
16 N	17 E	18 C	K	T	I	E		19 T	W	E	L	V	E	U	
G	O			20 W	R	21 A	D	I	O			A		L	
	O			O		R		E			22 K	N	I	V	E	S
	K			R		E		S		A			E		E
			23 R	O	B	E	S	O	N		T			R		N
			A			S			R		I			S	
			F				24 M	A	P		E				
25 H	O	L	T	Z	E	R		H							

Across
1. Derek admired Brian's
4. ____ bark; used for food containers
7. Derek's medical state
9. Bill____ said the government wanted Brian to teach them
10. Possible food
16. Name of the river
19. Pounds Brian lost
20. Left behind on trip down the river
22. Their only tools
23. Brian ____; two-time wilderness survivor
24. Showed the way to the trading post
25. Derek ____; psychologist who went with Brian

Down
2. Speed in mph the raft traveled
3. Months for Derek to recover
4. Name of trading post
5. Mr. ____; was about to get married
6. Caused the problems on the trip
7. Dangerous, rocky water
8. Needed to make a fire
9. Attacked the first night
11. Brian said there could never be too much of it
12. First Food
13. Months after trip when Brian received Derek's gift
14. Author
15. Cut the trees that Brian used for the raft
17. Brian's new hobby after first time in the wilderness
18. Katie ____; Brian and Derek's code name
21. ____ McKenzie; Brian's girlfriend
22. ____ ONE; radio station code name
23. Name of the canoe

MATCHING QUIZ/WORKSHEET 1 - The River

___ 1. CANOE A. ____ONE; radio station code name
___ 2. BOUGHS B. Contained the map, notebooks, and radio
___ 3. FIFTEEN C. Mr. ____ was about to get married.
___ 4. KATIE D. Derek's medical state
___ 5. TENSION E. Name of trading post
___ 6. RASPBERRIES F. Needed to make a fire
___ 7. MAP G. Brian's age during the trip
___ 8. COOK H. Derek admired Brian's
___ 9. CHUTE I. Dangerous, rocky water
___10. BRANNOCK J. It was 'everything' in the wild, according to Brian.
___11. BALLARD K. Pounds Brian lost
___12. RAFT L. Months for Derek to recover
___13. BIRCH M. Erik ____; government survival instructor
___14. COMA N. Caused the problems on the trip
___15. WOOD O. Brian said there could never be too much of it.
___16. BRIEFCASE P. Gift to Brian from Derek
___17. ROBESON Q. Pine ____; used for their beds
___18. FOOD R. First Food
___19. TWELVE S. Brian's new hobby after first time in the wilderness
___20. KNIVES T. Bill____ said the government wanted Brian to teach them.
___21. SIX U. The first part of the trip lacked it.
___22. ETHICS V. Showed the way to the trading post
___23. FLINT W. Their only tools
___24. LIGHTNING X. ____bark; used for food containers
___25. MANNERLY Y. Name of the canoe

KEY: MATCHING QUIZ/WORKSHEET 1 - The River

P - 1.	CANOE	A. ____ONE; radio station code name
Q - 2.	BOUGHS	B. Contained the map, notebooks, and radio
G - 3.	FIFTEEN	C. Mr. ____ was about to get married.
A - 4.	KATIE	D. Derek's medical state
U - 5.	TENSION	E. Name of trading post
R - 6.	RASPBERRIES	F. Needed to make a fire
V - 7.	MAP	G. Brian's age during the trip
S - 8.	COOK	H. Derek admired Brian's
I - 9.	CHUTE	I. Dangerous, rocky water
E -10.	BRANNOCK	J. It was 'everything' in the wild, according to Brian.
M -11.	BALLARD	K. Pounds Brian lost
Y -12.	RAFT	L. Months for Derek to recover
X -13.	BIRCH	M. Erik ____; government survival instructor
D -14.	COMA	N. Caused the problems on the trip
O -15.	WOOD	O. Brian said there could never be too much of it.
B -16.	BRIEFCASE	P. Gift to Brian from Derek
C -17.	ROBESON	Q. Pine ____; used for their beds
J -18.	FOOD	R. First Food
K -19.	TWELVE	S. Brian's new hobby after first time in the wilderness
W 20.	KNIVES	T. Bill____ said the government wanted Brian to teach them.
L -21.	SIX	U. The first part of the trip lacked it.
H -22.	ETHICS	V. Showed the way to the trading post
F -23.	FLINT	W. Their only tools
N -24.	LIGHTNING	X. ____bark; used for food containers
T -25.	MANNERLY	Y. Name of the canoe

MATCHING QUIZ/WORKSHEET 2 - The River

___ 1. GRUBWORMS   A. Dangerous, rocky water

___ 2. BRANNOCK   B. Months for Derek to recover

___ 3. CANOE   C. It was 'everything' in the wild, according to Brian.

___ 4. ETHICS   D. First Food

___ 5. NECKTIE   E. Two-time wilderness survivor

___ 6. COMA   F. Katie ____; Brian and Derek's code name

___ 7. WOOD   G. Name of trading post

___ 8. SIX   H. Brian said there could never be too much of it.

___ 9. DEBORAH   I. ____McKenzie; Brian's girlfriend

___ 10. BALLARD   J. Possible food

___ 11. CHUTE   K. Derek ____; psychologist who went with Brian

___ 12. JACKET   L. Derek admired Brian's

___ 13. HOLTZER   M. Gift to Brian from Derek

___ 14. BRIAN   N. Name of the canoe

___ 15. MAP   O. Kind of gear left behind in the plane

___ 16. COOK   P. Name of the river

___ 17. HUNGER   Q. Showed the way to the trading post

___ 18. BIRCH   R. Erik ____; government survival instructor

___ 19. RAFT   S. Brian used it to make strips.

___ 20. TWO   T. Pine ____; used for their beds

___ 21. FOOD   U. ____bark; used for food containers

___ 22. PAULSEN   V. Brian's worst problem during The Time

___ 23. BOUGHS   W. Brian's new hobby after first time in the wilderness

___ 24. SURVIVAL   X. Derek's medical state

___ 25. RASPBERRIES   Y. Author

KEY: MATCHING QUIZ/WORKSHEET 2 - The River

J - 1. GRUBWORMS	A.	Dangerous, rocky water
G - 2. BRANNOCK	B.	Months for Derek to recover
M - 3. CANOE	C.	It was 'everything' in the wild, according to Brian.
L - 4. ETHICS	D.	First Food
P - 5. NECKTIE	E.	Two-time wilderness survivor
X - 6. COMA	F.	Katie ____; Brian and Derek's code name
H - 7. WOOD	G.	Name of trading post
B - 8. SIX	H.	Brian said there could never be too much of it.
I - 9. DEBORAH	I.	____McKenzie; Brian's girlfriend
R -10. BALLARD	J.	Possible food
A -11. CHUTE	K.	Derek ____; psychologist who went with Brian
S -12. JACKET	L.	Derek admired Brian's
K -13. HOLTZER	M.	Gift to Brian from Derek
E -14. BRIAN	N.	Name of the canoe
Q -15. MAP	O.	Kind of gear left behind in the plane
W 16. COOK	P.	Name of the river
V -17. HUNGER	Q.	Showed the way to the trading post
U -18. BIRCH	R.	Erik ____; government survival instructor
N -19. RAFT	S.	Brian used it to make strips.
F -20. TWO	T.	Pine ____; used for their beds
C -21. FOOD	U.	____bark; used for food containers
Y -22. PAULSEN	V.	Brian's worst problem during The Time
T -23. BOUGHS	W.	Brian's new hobby after first time in the wilderness
O -24. SURVIVAL	X.	Derek's medical state
D -25. RASPBERRIES	Y.	Author

WORD SCRAMBLE GAME *The River*

EBRVASE	BEAVERS	cut the trees that Brian used for the raft
RICHRABBK	BIRCH BARK	used for food containers
ARNOBCNK	BRANNOCK	name of trading post
INRORONBASEB	BRIAN ROBESON	two-time wilderness survivor
CIFAEREBS	BRIEFCASE	contained the map, notebooks, and radio
OCEAN	CANOE	gift to Brian form Derek
TECHU	CHUTE	dangerous, rocky water
MOCA	COMA	Derek's medical state
CLOOERUNS	COUNSELOR	thought Brian was mentally injured
REOHZDLETERK	DEREK HOLTZER	psychologist who went with Brian
HTIESC	ETHICS	Derek admired Brian's
REIF	FIRE	they didn't have one the first night
NLIFT	FLINT	needed to make a fire
DOFO	FOOD	was "everything" in the wild, according to Brian
PAYANUGLSRE	GARY PAULSEN	author
MGBWUORRS	GRUBWORMS	possible food
RUNHGE	HUNGER	Brian's worst problem during The Time
AKJETC	JACKET	Brian used it to make strips
EATONEIK	KATIE ONE	radio station code name
WATIETOK	KATIE TWO	Brian and Derek's code name
SKIEVN	KNIVES	their only tools
GIHNTNIGL	LIGHTNING	caused the problems on the trip
QOSUITOMES	MOSQUITOES	attacked the first night
ECNTIEK	NECKTIE	name of the river
INGEBPUHSO	PINE BOUGHS	used for their beds
OLARPP	POPLAR	trees used for the raft
DAIRO	RADIO	left behind on trip down the river
ATFR	RAFT	name of the canoe
SPRBEARISRE	RASPBERRIES	first food
VASURVILAREG	SURVIVAL GEAR	left behind in the plane
OTSINEN	TENSION	the first part of the trip lacked it
MHETIET	THE TIME	Brian's name for his first wilderness experience
DOWO	WOOD	Brian said there could never be too much of it

VOCABULARY RESOURCES

The River Vocabulary Word Search

```
A C C U R A T E G H T H R I V E L T Y
R E C T I F Y N M H C B N G N Q R C L
A S P E C T I V N L E Y M H N E Y H E
V O W E D Y D H E M V L A D V N H U S
E P B D R D S U H N O N M E N O C T R
S G U P D K Q S H J C N R N O I S E E
I N F J E S L V M E L O B O I T K Q V
M I F M R V Z P D D A I H O T A I N R
O N E K E P E C E H Z T G R A C M E E
R E T D B M V T R Q M U V A R I P G P
P E E Y M S N F O U B A Q M E D Y A F
M R D G A E L G C E D C N W P N Q T D
O A S G L U R C H E D E V A S I V E T
C C S E C A F P R E D R S T A T D D G
M G R S M F Z L X R S P B J X D T L R
S U V Y I X I E O S T U N N E D B M A
D K T Y X V L H D V O E L B A T S M T
R Y N E N F E L Y D G N M K M V O B S
F Y F A D N E F M M S E C K Q C Z F F
```

ACCURATE	CRUDE	HORDE	RECTIFY
ALCOVE	CUE	INDICATION	RELENTED
ANVIL	DOUBTS	LURCHED	REVERT
ASPECT	EMBEDDED	MAROONED	SKIMPY
BUFFETED	ENHANCED	MASSIVE	SQUELCH
CAREENING	EVASIVE	MUTED	STABLE
CHUTE	EXASPERATION	NEGATED	STUNNED
CLAMBERED	FEND	PERVERSELY	THRIVE
COMA	FLEXED	PRECAUTION	VETOED
COMPROMISE	GLAZED	PRYING	VOWED

The River Vocabulary Word Search Answer Key

```
A C C U R A T E G    T H R I V E      T
R E C T I F Y N      C       N    R   L
A S P E C T I        L E     H    E   H
V O W E D Y     E    V   A D V    N   U
E   B   R   U        O   N   N    O C T
S G U P D   Q        C N R   O I  S E
I N F   E S       E L O   O  T K  E
M I F   R V     D D A I   O  A I  N
O N F   E   E C     T R   T  C M  E
R E T   B     T R   U A   I  I P  G
P E     M   N   O   A M   E  D Y  A
M R D G A E       E D C   P  N    T D
O A   L U R C H E D E V A S I V E
C C S E C       E D R   T A   D   D
M   R S   Z L X R   P B   X D
    U   I   E O S T U N N E D         A
      T   V L H D   O E L B A T S M
        E N F E     D       M     O
        A D N E F           E     C
```

ACCURATE	CRUDE	HORDE	RECTIFY
ALCOVE	CUE	INDICATION	RELENTED
ANVIL	DOUBTS	LURCHED	REVERT
ASPECT	EMBEDDED	MAROONED	SKIMPY
BUFFETED	ENHANCED	MASSIVE	SQUELCH
CAREENING	EVASIVE	MUTED	STABLE
CHUTE	EXASPERATION	NEGATED	STUNNED
CLAMBERED	FEND	PERVERSELY	THRIVE
COMA	FLEXED	PRECAUTION	VETOED
COMPROMISE	GLAZED	PRYING	VOWED

The River Vocabulary Crossword Puzzle

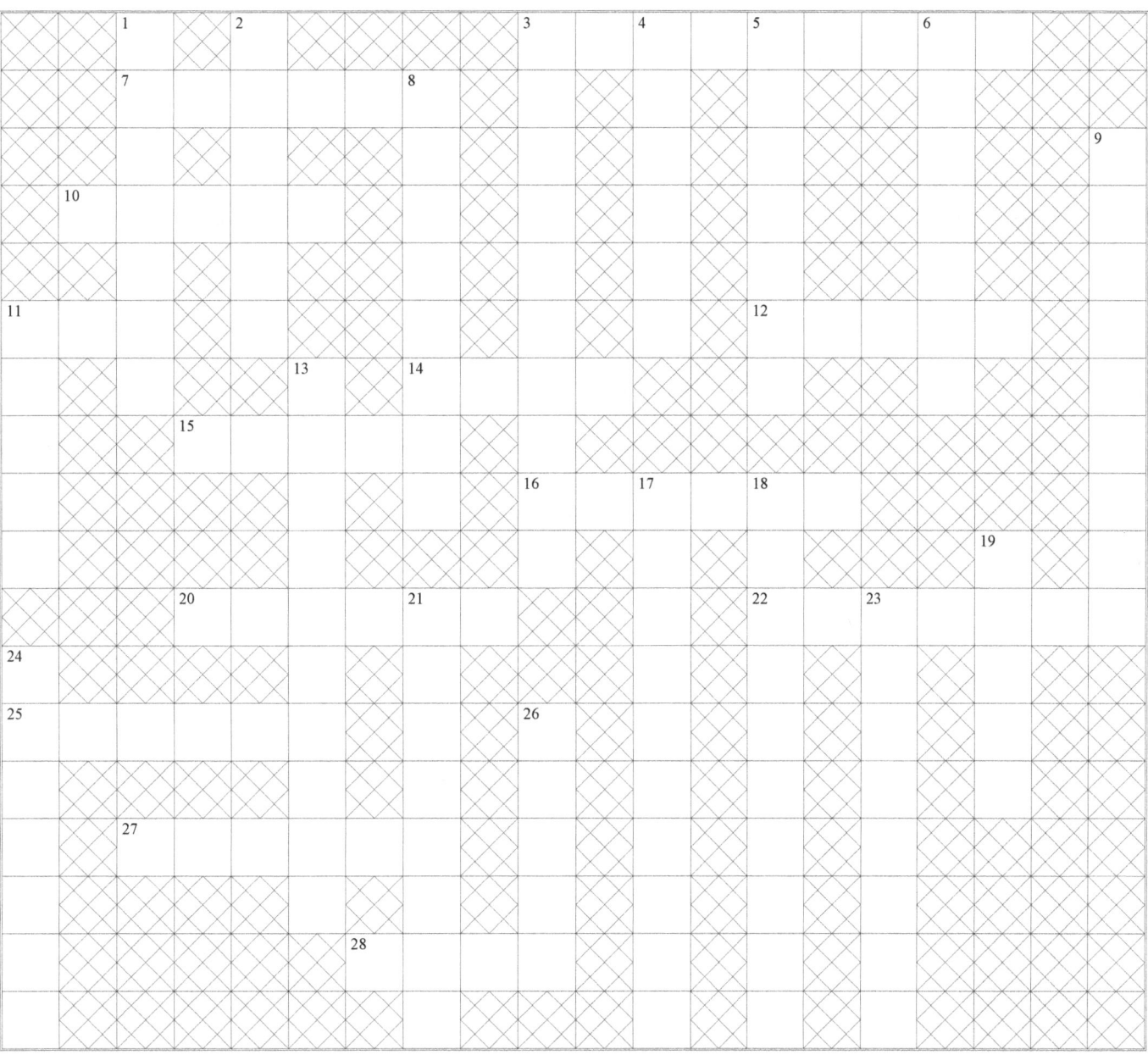

Across
- 3. Rushing headlong
- 7. Succeed
- 10. Heavy block of iron or steal
- 11. Sign
- 12. Promised
- 14. Unconsciousness
- 15. A large group; swarm
- 16. Not enough; inadequate
- 20. Glassy eyed
- 22. rolled; dipped down
- 25. Way of looking at something
- 27. Rejected; refused
- 28. Fight against

Down
- 1. Shocked
- 2. Looking curiously; snooping
- 3. Agreement
- 4. To return to a former condition
- 5. Misleading
- 6. Ruled out
- 8. Improved
- 9. covered with water
- 11. Roughly made
- 13. Safeguard
- 17. sign; signal
- 18. Ground to powder or dust
- 19. A waterfall; a channel
- 21. firmly enclosed
- 23. Eased off
- 24. Enormous
- 26. Muffled; softened

The River Vocabulary Crossword Puzzle Answer Key

		1 S		2 P				3 C	4 A	5 R	E	E	6 N	I	N	G	
		7 T	H	R	I	V	8 E		O		E		V		E		
		U		Y			N		M		V		A		G		9 S
	10 A	N	V	I	L		H		P		E		S		A		U
		N		N			A		R		R		I		T		B
11 C	U	E		G			N		O		12 T		V	O	W	E	D	M
R		D			13 P		14 C	O	M	A			E		D		E
U			15 H	O	R	D	E		I								R
D					E		D		16 S	K	17 I	M	18 P	Y			G
E					C				E		N		U			19 C	E
			20 G	L	A	21 Z	E	D			D		22 L	U	23 R	C	H	E	D
24 M					U		M				I		V		E		U		
25 A	S	P	E	C	T		B		26 M		C		E		L		T		
S					I		E		U		A		R		E		E		
S		27 V	E	T	O	E	D		T		T		I		N				
I					N		D		E		I		Z		T				
V						28 F	E	N	D		O		E		E				
E						D					N		D		D				

Across
3. Rushing headlong
7. Succeed
10. Heavy block of iron or steal
11. Sign
12. Promised
14. Unconsciousness
15. A large group; swarm
16. Not enough; inadequate
20. Glassy eyed
22. rolled; dipped down
25. Way of looking at something
27. Rejected; refused
28. Fight against

Down
1. Shocked
2. Looking curiously; snooping
3. Agreement
4. To return to a former condition
5. Misleading
6. Ruled out
8. Improved
9. covered with water
11. Roughly made
13. Safeguard
17. sign; signal
18. Ground to powder or dust
19. A waterfall; a channel
21. firmly enclosed
23. Eased off
24. Enormous
26. Muffled; softened

VOCABULARY WORKSHEET 1 - The River

___ 1. DISINTEGRATE   A. Heavy block of iron or steel
___ 2. MUTED   B. Sign
___ 3. HORDE   C. Rolled; dipped down
___ 4. PERVERSELY   D. Rejected; refused
___ 5. RECTIFY   E. Way of looking at something
___ 6. CHUTE   F. A large group; swarm
___ 7. MASSIVE   G. Glassy-eyed
___ 8. STABLE   H. To set right; correct
___ 9. RELENTED   I. Rushing headlong
___10. VETOED   J. Hit; beat
___11. ALCOVE   K. Not enough; inadequate
___12. ANVIL   L. Wrongly stubborn
___13. BUFFETED   M. An indentation or small hollow
___14. SQUELCH   N. Enormous
___15. DEHYDRATION   O. To fall apart
___16. STUNNED   P. A waterfall; a channel
___17. PULVERIZED   Q. Ground to powder or dust
___18. GLAZED   R. Shocked
___19. CAREENING   S. To silence
___20. LURCHED   T. Sturdy
___21. EXTERNALIZE   U. Loss of water or moisture
___22. VOWED   V. Muffled; softened
___23. SKIMPY   W. Eased off
___24. ASPECT   X. To show outwardly
___25. CUE   Y. Promised

KEY: VOCABULARY WORKSHEET 1 - The River

O - 1.	DISINTEGRATE	A. Heavy block of iron or steel
V - 2.	MUTED	B. Sign
F - 3.	HORDE	C. Rolled; dipped down
L - 4.	PERVERSELY	D. Rejected; refused
H - 5.	RECTIFY	E. Way of looking at something
P - 6.	CHUTE	F. A large group; swarm
N - 7.	MASSIVE	G. Glassy-eyed
T - 8.	STABLE	H. To set right; correct
W - 9.	RELENTED	I. Rushing headlong
D - 10.	VETOED	J. Hit; beat
M - 11.	ALCOVE	K. Not enough; inadequate
A - 12.	ANVIL	L. Wrongly stubborn
J - 13.	BUFFETED	M. An indentation or small hollow
S - 14.	SQUELCH	N. Enormous
U - 15.	DEHYDRATION	O. To fall apart
R - 16.	STUNNED	P. A waterfall; a channel
Q - 17.	PULVERIZED	Q. Ground to powder or dust
G - 18.	GLAZED	R. Shocked
I - 19.	CAREENING	S. To silence
C - 20.	LURCHED	T. Sturdy
X - 21.	EXTERNALIZE	U. Loss of water or moisture
Y - 22.	VOWED	V. Muffled; softened
K - 23.	SKIMPY	W. Eased off
E - 24.	ASPECT	X. To show outwardly
B - 25.	CUE	Y. Promised

VOCABULARY WORKSHEET 2 - The River

___ 1. FLEXED   A. Rushing headlong
___ 2. REVERT   B. Hit; beat
___ 3. GLAZED   C. Unconsciousness
___ 4. PRECAUTION   D. Ruled out
___ 5. NEGATED   E. Glassy-eyed
___ 6. PERVERSELY   F. Shocked
___ 7. VETOED   G. Wrongly stubborn
___ 8. CAREENING   H. Eased off
___ 9. COMA   I. A waterfall; a channel
___10. SUBMERGED   J. Heavy block of iron or steel
___11. BUFFETED   K. Uncertainties
___12. EVASIVE   L. Roughly made
___13. COMPROMISE   M. To set right; correct
___14. ANVIL   N. A large group; swarm
___15. STUNNED   O. Safeguard
___16. HORDE   P. Not enough; inadequate
___17. RECTIFY   Q. Misleading; avoiding
___18. INDICATION   R. Agreement
___19. EMBEDDED   S. Rejected; refused
___20. DOUBTS   T. Covered with water
___21. SKIMPY   U. Bent
___22. CHUTE   V. To show outwardly
___23. RELENTED   W. To return to a former condition
___24. CRUDE   X. Sign; signal
___25. EXTERNALIZE   Y. Firmly enclosed

KEY: VOCABULARY WORKSHEET 2 - The River

U - 1.	FLEXED	A. Rushing headlong
W - 2.	REVERT	B. Hit; beat
E - 3.	GLAZED	C. Unconsciousness
O - 4.	PRECAUTION	D. Ruled out
D - 5.	NEGATED	E. Glassy-eyed
G - 6.	PERVERSELY	F. Shocked
S - 7.	VETOED	G. Wrongly stubborn
A - 8.	CAREENING	H. Eased off
C - 9.	COMA	I. A waterfall; a channel
T - 10.	SUBMERGED	J. Heavy block of iron or steel
B - 11.	BUFFETED	K. Uncertainties
Q - 12.	EVASIVE	L. Roughly made
R - 13.	COMPROMISE	M. To set right; correct
J - 14.	ANVIL	N. A large group; swarm
F - 15.	STUNNED	O. Safeguard
N - 16.	HORDE	P. Not enough; inadequate
M - 17.	RECTIFY	Q. Misleading; avoiding
X - 18.	INDICATION	R. Agreement
Y - 19.	EMBEDDED	S. Rejected; refused
K - 20.	DOUBTS	T. Covered with water
P - 21.	SKIMPY	U. Bent
I - 22.	CHUTE	V. To show outwardly
H - 23.	RELENTED	W. To return to a former condition
L - 24.	CRUDE	X. Sign; signal
V - 25.	EXTERNALIZE	Y. Firmly enclosed

VOCABULARY WORD SCRAMBLE *The River*

TAUERCAC	ACCURATE	exact
LAOEVC	ALCOVE	an indentation or small hollow
VAILN	ANVIL	heavy block of iron or steel
PEVTCA	ASPECT	way of looking at something
FEUTFEDB	BUFFETED	hit; beat
NAECGNERI	CAREENING	rushing headlong
TCUEH	CHUTE	a waterfall; a channel
LARBECEDM	CLAMBERED	climbed
AMOC	COMA	unconsciousness
MOPOISRECM	COMPROMISE	agreement
RCDEU	CRUDE	roughly made
UEC	CUE	sign
DYDTARIOENH	DEHYDRATION	loss of water or moisture
IIRNTEGSDATE	DISINTEGRATE	to fall apart
BOTDUS	DOUBTS	uncertainties
DMEEDBED	EMBEDDED	firmly enclosed
HEEACDNN	ENHANCED	improved
SEAVIEV	EVASIVE	misleading
SAXOPERATIEN	EXASPERATION	annoyance
TENAIZEXERL	EXTERNALIZE	to show outwardly
NDEF	FEND	fight against
ELEXDF	FLEXED	bent
LAEDGZ	GLAZED	glassy eyed
DOREH	HORDE	a large group; swarm
ANITDIIONC	INDICATION	sign; signal
HUREDLC	LURCHED	rolled; dipped down
OMAROEDN	MAROONED	abandoned
SSIEMAV	MASSIVE	enormous
UEDMT	MUTED	muffled; softened
EEATDNG	NEGATED	ruled out
YERERPSELV	PERVERSELY	wrongly stubborn
ENCAROUPTI	PRECAUTION	safeguard
RNYIGP	PRYING	looking curiously; snooping
ZURLEIEDPV	PULVERIZED	ground to powder or dust
RTYIFCE	RECTIFY	to set right; correct
DREETLEN	RELENTED	eased off
EVRTRE	REVERT	to return to a former condition
MSKYIP	SKIMPY	not enough; inadequate
QLSCUEH	SQUELCH	to silence

TBALES	STABLE	sturdy
SUNTEDN	STUNNED	shocked
BUGSDREEM	SUBMERGED	covered with water
HIVRET	THRIVE	succeed
ETODE V	VETOED	rejected; refused
EOWVD	VOWED	promised